The S ... was Told:
Short Stories of Abbeyleix
By Noel Burke
Photography by James G. Carroll
Edited by Ruby Eyre

Photography by James G Carroll
Book Cover design by Jessica Whelan (Author's Granddaughter)
Edited by Ruby Eyre

ISBN: 978-1-3999-4095-5

When you sit, ponder, and reflect back on your life living and growing up in Abbeyleix – why not document a story about a memory that stands out in your mind, so that it can be passed on to the generations to follow? When you get to a stage in life where you like to look back on the life you have lived, it is lovely to recall memories of people that you knew and the stories that they told. Preserve the past for the future.

– Noel Burke

For my father.

Author's Note

While writing this book, I was privileged to learn so much about our beautiful Heritage Town of Abbeyleix. A considerable amount of information was uncovered, during my attempt to piece together and write this book, with the help of James G Carroll, photographer, who captured the images that were so important for hopefully making this a successful project for us. The information was scattered around in lots of books, pamphlets, and papers of every description. I was always fascinated by our local history, I wanted to know where I came from, and how the town came to be here. I wanted to interview all the old characters that lived in our town, collect, and document the stories that they told.

It occurred to me at a young age that this is something that I should be doing. I'm not quite sure when my interest was sparked, but I do recall that my own father loved to tell old stories when we were young, lots of them Ghost stories. I believe now that this was an attempt to get us to go to bed early and stay there once, we were in it, because we would be afraid to stick our head above the blankets in case there was a Ghost lurking about.

This book is not intended to be a definitive history of Abbeyleix, that will be left to more learned and professional historians. What it is, is an attempt to recall and recreate, in some small way, the life and times of those who lived in Abbeyleix throughout the years.

Some of the stories in this book are based on the historical data of historians of the past as well as a couple of present-day historians like Kevin P. O. Brien, from Killamuck and Michael Lynch, from Ballytarsna. This book, although based on information gathered from historians, has a narrative that is interwoven with lore and legend as well as facts, passed down through the years to make the reading of the stories as enjoyable as it may be informative.

- Noel Burke-

End of an Era

As I write this, it was March 2021. A sad day for Abbeyleix and particularly, for the Ryan family. It is the end of an era. The Ryan family have been in business in Abbeyleix for more than 124 years. We, the people of Abbeyleix, are sad to see it go. When an event like this happens in a town, the memories come flooding back and reminds us all just how short our lives really are.

In the photo, Karen Ryan and Betty Whelan are closing the doors of the shop for the last time. Betty has been associated with this business for many years, along with Sophie Hinchin. Karen's mother, Mrs Phil Ryan, also shown in the photo standing beside Sophie are sadly no longer with us today. Rest in Peace to both.

The Ryan family have had a presence in business on Main Street Abbeyleix dating back to 1896. Patrick Ryan, hailing from Co. Tipperary, served his apprenticeship to the trade with William J. Morrissey and following that he started his own business two doors up the street. A photograph taken in 1906 shows a Drapery shop and a general store, as was

common to Abbeyleix at the time. A bakery also operated from the rear of the property. Of historical interest, Patrick Ryan was an Agent for The White Star Line. A ticket for the ill-fated Titanic was purchased by a man called William Henry Gillespie who was lost to sea when the Titanic sank in 1912. In his memory, a gravestone was erected in the graveyard in the Church of Ireland, Abbeyleix.

After Patrick Ryan died in 1955 his Daughter Mary Ryan continued to operate a general store Newsagents until the property was sold to Moran's in the mid-1960s. In 1965 May Ryan bought the adjoining Main Street premises, known as 'Mercier's', which included a drapery shop known as 'Nolan's'. Alongside this was a hairdresser and a coffee shop. Mrs Ryan opened the coffee shop as an alternative option for the sale of refreshments on fair day. She later opened 'The Gift Shop' where it is currently located in the 1970s selling as advertised, cards, confectionery, and chocolate.

After her death in December 1977, her sister-in-law Mrs. Phil Ryan took over in 1978 first dispensing with the sale of confectionery and chocolate and concentrating on a gift shop which she ran for the next 42 years until her passing on 5th April 2020. It is for sure the end of an era.

The Tunduff Ambush 1922.

On Thursday evening, the 28th of July 2022, a large crowd gathered near Coole, Raheen to remember the men that had lost their lives when shots were fired in what has become known as the Tunduff Ambush.

The Anglo-Irish Treaty was signed in Downing Street, London on the 6th of December 1921. The agreement became effective on the 31st of March 1922. The Irish Free State thus created became fully implemented on the 6th of December 1922.

Unrest swept the Country which started three years before the Easter Rising in 1916. The War of Independence followed lasting just over 2 years starting in January 1919 and into early July 1921.The signing of the Anglo-Irish Treaty in 1921 was effectively the beginning of the Irish Civil War which changed everything.

People who had the same goal and fought on the same side against the occupying forces during the Easter Rising and continued to fight on the same side during the War of Independence, began to split and take opposing sides. Irish people took different viewpoints regarding the signing of the

Treaty, even causing a rift within families. This was truly a horrible time for the Irish People.

On the 27th of June 1922, Michael Collins gave a final ultimatum to the four courts garrison to surrender before they were attacked. Collins borrowed two British 18-pounder field guns to bombard the Four Courts beginning at 4.15am, marking the definitive start of the Irish Civil War. This was a very emotive time in our history. But no matter which side of the fence you were on, this is still our past and our history and we must own it.

The Ambush Site

A family by the name of Dobbs lived in a house about half a mile from Abbeyleix at the time. The owners of this house are now known to us today as Bennetts of Tunduff who owned the site chosen for the ambush on the 28th of July 1922. The site was picked for its high garden wall at the front of the house and its close location to the main road.

The family home had been taken over by the Irregulars (as they were known as) at the time. Their intention was to remain there in place until the convoy of Free State soldiers had made their way to the ambush site. The Dobbs family said that they were always treated well by the people that had taken over their house. Herbert Dobbs remained living in the house until he decided to move his family up to the North of Ireland in the late 1930s. Herbert also remarked that Michael Collins visited the family home shortly after the ambush and apologised to the family for being caught up in this incident.

Michael Sheehy, a leader of one of the republican columns that day, gave his account of the ambush on Friday afternoon, the 28th of July. The ambush site prepared for a Free State convoy of armoured cars travelling from Kilkenny through Abbeyleix. The convoy were headed towards Portlaoise with arms and money for the soldiers occupying the barracks there. The information that the Irregulars were in possession of was that the convoy of Free State soldiers were to pass through Abbeyleix in the early hours of the morning. About twenty rifle men and three engineers cycled fourteen miles from their base in the Slieve Bloom Mountains during the night to the Tunduff ambush site.

Two 14lb mines were placed in the middle of the road buried approximately 3 ft deep close to both ends of the wall. The mines had been transported from Portarlington to Tunduff earlier that morning. The plan was that the convoy was to be allowed to pass over the first mine unhindered and when the armoured car was over the second mine, both mines were to be detonated pinning down the soldiers in their vehicles.

Ambush Site

Forewarned

A report had been received in Portlaoise barracks that mines were located between Tunduff Cross and Abbeyleix town. Captain Joubert F. Powell was sent out in charge of a party to remove the mines. The party consisted of rifle men in two lorries preceded by a Lancia car bearing a Lewis gun team along with Brigadier Mick Gray.

When the Lancia car reached the first mine, it was detonated resulting in the car being blown up and landing on its side after it already had thrown the soldiers clear of the vehicle. The soldiers were then attacked with rifle fire and hand grenades. One soldier named Thomas Grace from Mountrath had tried to retrieve his rifle from the side of the road when he was shot dead. Four other soldiers were wounded at the scene including Mick Gray. Thomas Grace survived the First World

War as a British soldier, a war that had ended in 1918, but Tunduff became the place where his life was cut short.

Commandant Berry captured two men along with their weapons in the house close by. The rest of the ambush party retreated from the front garden of the house. They travelled along the old bog road along by the side of the wood, and then through a hay field where they arrived at a sandpit near Coole Cross, Raheen. This is where the Irregulars took cover and waited for the Free State soldiers to follow. Food was stored in a potato field close to the sandpit, suggesting that the Irregulars were expecting to be in that area for some time.

View from behind the Garden Wall.

Reinforcements on the Way

Once word of the ambush reached the barracks in Portlaoise, reinforcements were sent out under the command of Colonel Commandant Austin MacCurtin and Commandant M.F. Gantley. Colonel Commandant John Collison of Roscrea, who happened to be in Portlaoise at the time, joined the party. These forces were deployed across the country in the direction of Abbeyleix. John had been an IRA commander in the North Tipperary Flying Column's during the War of Independence. Comdt. MacCurtin, Comdt. Collinson, and Captain Powell searched the land near Coole, Raheen with the main body going another way. Comdt. Ganley with another party, were some distance away moving in a circle to join Comdt. MacCurtin. Hearing a burst of gun fire in the direction of Comdt. MacCurtin, Comdt Ganley moved towards them and found eight Irregulars in a field with their hands up. Behind a ditch nearby, ten Irregulars surrendered with Comdts. Collinson, MacCurtin and Captain Powell lying on the ground wounded. Captain Joubert Powell was shot in the face, staggered backwards, and fell into a ditch where he lay for quite a long time. The Irregulars behind the ditch waited until the party were close before firing a volley of shots at them. Abandoning their weapons, they put up their hands and came forward calling for mercy. The local clergy was then sent for. Fr. Coyne P.P. of Raheen and Fr. Dunne promptly attended and administered the last Sacraments to the wounded officers. Comdt. MacCurtin died just after receiving the Sacraments. Several Free State soldiers were sent to the nearest house to acquire a stretcher so that they could carry the wounded officers as well as the body of Comdt MacCurtin away for medical assistance. The soldiers arrived at the house near Coole Cross belonging to a family by the name of Kelly. They asked the woman of the house if they could take the door off the shed so that they could use it as an improvised stretcher. Mrs Kelly directed them away from the shed and showed them a ladder which they could use as a stretcher for the wounded men. The soldiers took the ladder without ever knowing the shed was used to store the bicycles of the Irregulars that took part in the ambush at Tunduff.

County Infirmary, Portlaoise

Just as Comdt. John (Jack) Collison had been brought into the Infirmary in Portlaoise, which was directly opposite the Prison, he died from the wounds that he had received at the Tunduff Ambush. Subsequently, as many as twenty-one Irregulars were rounded up and marched back to Portlaoise Prison, where they were officially arrested on the 29th of July 1922. The men were held in solitary confinement in 'A' wing by order of Comdt. Ganley. The Irregulars that were caught came from areas all over Co Laois. From places including Abbeyleix, Portlaoise, Portarlington, Mountmellick, Clonaslee, Ballickmoyler,

Tinnahinch Clarahill, Clonaheen, Rosenallis, and Wolfhill. Several of the leaders of the Irregulars made their escape apart from Michael Sheehy who was also arrested after most of the column had been captured at the scene of the shooting.

My final thoughts on the Tunduff Ambush

The 28th of July 1922 was and is an important date in our history and it is only right that the soldiers that had lost their lives at the Tunduff Ambush should be remembered now 100 years on and continue to be recognised and remembered from now and into the future for the sacrifices that they had made. Mike Rafter must be thanked in the first instance for all the hard work that he has invested bringing our past history to life. The hours, days, weeks, and months spent researching the history, culminating a 2nd Edition book that he published entitled *The Quiet County*. The period of Irish history he has covered was from 1913-1923.Denis Collison from Tipperary who has two sons living in Abbeyleix and indeed his family have played a major role in safeguarding our past by erecting this magnificent monument at Coole Raheen in remembrance of those fallen soldiers. Donal and Anne Tynan also need to be thanked for donating a portion of their own property, and at their own expense for the erection of this beautiful piece of Art in memory

of the men that lost their lives at the Tunduff Ambush.

I have lived in Abbeyleix all my life and have never heard anybody speak about what happened at Tunduff in 1922. For obvious reasons I can understand why families didn't want to talk about those events back then. After all, it was a Civil War. Now that it is 100 years on from the 28th of July 1922, it surely is time that the people of our town, our county, and indeed our country should be made aware of just what happened here at Tunduff in Abbeyleix.

The Dobbs Family

Herbert, Margaret and George, 1936

The Dobbs Family lived in the house used in the Tunduff Ambush. The house is often referred to as Tunduff Park. It is now owned by the Bennett family.

Letitia Dobbs, her son Herbert, and daughter Ina Mary lived in the Tunduff house. During the Irish Civil War, the house was used as an ambush site by several Irregulars on the 28th of July 1922. The Irregulars planned to ambush a convoy of Free State soldiers en route to Portlaoise. The ambush did not work out in the way it had been intended. Nevertheless, three Irish Free State soldiers lost their lives and a number of them were seriously injured. This incident has become known as the Tunduff Ambush.

As we try to tell the story of the family using images of the people that we are writing about, the following is a summary of the pictures we have of the Dobbs family. James and I firmly believe in the old saying that 'A Picture Paints a Thousand Words'.

The picture above is of Herbert and his wife Margaret with their son George taken in 1936 just before they sold their house and moved to Belfast in the North of Ireland. Herbert's father, Joe Dobbs, was a businessman in Abbeyleix who has been described as a 'trader.' Joe Dobbs owned several businesses in Abbeyleix, which included the premises that was later purchased by John Baggot in the late 1920s.

In the next picture, Herbert is wearing his Abbeyleix Preston School uniform, holding his pet dog. This photo was taken in 1914.

Herbert and his Dog 1914.

The Story Begins

No members of the Dobbs family live in Abbeyleix anymore, but the family name stills survive through the headstones at the Church of Ireland and that of the old Church graveyard on the Abbeyleix Estate. The Dobbs family arrived in Ireland as Cromwellian army officers around 1650 and acquired land first in Cranemore in Carlow. Incidentally, this is where John Baggot hailed from as well, before coming to Abbeyleix and purchasing Joe Dobbs's furniture and grocery shop at lower main street in the town. A section of the Dobbs family moved to Abbeyleix in the 18th century while some moved to Castlecomer, county Kilkenny, in the 19th century where they settled.

The Castlecomer branch became agents for the local landlords, the Wandesfordes Estate, that has now become better known as the Castlecomer Discovery Park. The Dobbs family lived in 'The Cottage.' Later, a few of them became clergymen while others married into nobility such as the Earls of Rosse.

The wife of the famous English writer Malcolm Muggerridge was Kitty Dobbs (1927-1990), who originally hailed from Castlecomer. Malcolm in his twenties was attracted to communism and went to live in the Soviet Union in the 1930s, and the experience turned him into an anti-communist.

The Abbeyleix Branch

Joseph Dobbs was born in 1771 in a little house on the Mountrath road that was called the Warren. His son Robert was born in 1842 who later became the father of Joseph Dobbs the Abbeyleix businesses man that lived in Tunduff Park. Joseph purchased Tunduff in 1890 and lived there with his wife Letitia and raised their five children – Annie Beatrice 'Bertie' (married Joseph Lalor from Ballygouge, Ballycolla), Letitia Evelyn (married Mr Herbert Carrington Laird from Belfast), Dinah 'Ina' Mary (unmarried), John Large (married Ruby Gillespie and moved to Greenmount, Abbeyleix) and Joseph 'Herbert' Conway (married Margaret 'Margo' Wheeler and inherited Tunduff Park).

This Dobbs family could rightfully be described as real Abbeyleix people as they were here before the 2nd Viscount, John De Vesci decided to demolish Old Town and create a new planned town on higher ground. The town was called New Rathmoyle, and then New Town at the time before eventually settling on the name Abbeyleix where I live today. The town was constructed in the late 1700s.

Joe Dobbs owned several farms around Abbeyleix at the time which included a farm on the Green Road now owned by the Cass family. He also owned a farm that was known as Greenmount situated between Blackhill and Ballytarsna on the Mountrath road, now also owned by a different branch of the Cass family. He also operated a business on the premises which later became known as John Baggot's furniture and grocery shop. It was situated at the lower end of Main Street in the town.

Joseph's son, John, inherited one of the farms from his father that was known as Greenmount when he married a lady by the name of Ruby Adelaide (née Gillespie) that hailed from Boyle in County Roscommon. Being interested in the equine business, John became a bloodstock breeder. He became involved in this business while living on the farm there. Both John and Ruby were keen members of the Queen's County Hunt, which formed in 1850 and later amalgamated with the Emo Hounds, now known as the Laois Hunt. John and Ruby Dobbs went on to have a son in which they named Joseph Alfred, born on December the 22nd 1914 who later in life became a diplomat and eventually became Britain's leading authority on the Soviet Union. Joe Dobbs married a woman named Marie (nee Catton) and went on to have four sons. Joe Dobbs, born in 1914, passed away on the 28th of September 2002.

Michael Dobbs

Michael Dobbs, a son of Joseph Alfred Dobbs and grandson of John Large Dobbs from Abbeyleix, is a best-selling, non-fiction author and journalist for the Washington Post. He wrote many articles on the Watergate scandal and covered the collapse of communism as a foreign correspondent. Michael was born in Belfast in 1950 and became a US citizen in 2010.

Leaving Abbeyleix

John and Ruby sold their businesses in Greenmount in the 1930s, leaving Abbeyleix for good. They moved to Daventry in England before returning to live in Glengormley just outside Belfast in 1946. John was born in 1886 and died in 1972. His wife Ruby Adelaide Dobbs (née Gillespie) was born 1892 and died in 1977.

Lord Michael Dobbs, author, and executive producer of *House of Cards*.

Lord Michael Dobbs, not to be confused with Michael Dobbs, (who is John Dobb's grandson) is a best-selling author educated in Britain, born in 1948 in Hertfordshire, England. A former Conservative politician and novelist. Michael Dobbs is best known for his *House of Cards* trilogy. He was also an advisor to Margaret Thatcher when the Conservatives were in power. Michael Dobbs returned to Abbeyleix where his ancestors are buried.

Servant burned to death in Abbeyleix house Inferno

In the early hours of the morning on the 11th of September 1915, the residence of Mrs. Letitia Dobbs, Tunduff Park, Abbeyleix, was destroyed by fire. The house was destroyed with only a few small articles saved. Mrs. Letitia Dobbs, her daughter Miss Ina Mary Dobbs, and their servant Bridget Gunn (née Coffey) were asleep in bed. Letitia's son, Master Herbert Dobbs, and a boy named Taylor were spending the night in a tent on the opposite side of the main road. It appears that at about 1 am in the morning, Mrs. Dobbs awakened by the sound of crackling timber coming from the servant's bedroom which was close to her one on the first floor.

Letitia Dobbs got up from her bed as quickly as she could. She went to the servant's bedroom, banged on the door, and began to shout her name with no response from Mrs. Gunn. Mrs. Dobbs tried to open the bedroom door only to be beaten back by smoke and flames from the fire. Quickly, she pulled the door shut and hurried down the landing to alert her daughter Ina Mary Dobbs. She called her daughter and told her to get out of the house quickly. Luckily both mother and daughter got out of the house in time uninjured.

Ina Mary alerted her brother Herbert and Taylor. The two young boys summoned help from people in the neighbourhood before cycling into Abbeyleix looking for further assistance. It was impossible, however, owing to the scarcity of water, to combat the flames. Efforts were made to save some items from the inferno, but very little was saved apart from a few small items. The following day a search was made in the debris for the remains of the servant, Mrs Gunn, but only a small portion of her body, badly charred was discovered. The residence was destroyed, only the bare blackened walls remained.

It was believed that the candle that the servant used to light up her room had somehow fallen over as she slept. Shortly after the fire, Mrs. Letitia Dobbs wrote to the Nationalist & Leinster Times and said that she wanted to thank her neighbours and friends for all their help during the tragic event at her home on the 11th of September 1915.

The following is a copy of the written letter that Mrs Letitia Dobbs wrote to the Editor of The Nationalist and Leinster Times:

Dear Sir----

Will you kindly allow me space in your journal to return my sincere thanks to all those that responded with such

promptitude to the call for help, and endeavoured to extinguish the fire at
Tunduff Park on the morning of the 10th instant. I desire specially to thank Head Constable Deignan and the members of the RIC, for their valuable assistance. I am deeply grateful for the letters and telegrams of sympathy received from numerous friends to whom I hope to reply individually---
Yours faithfully, Letitia Dobbs. Abbeyleix, September 16th, 1915.

Letitia Makes A Big Decision

Letitia Dobbs was faced with a huge decision that she had to make following the fire that destroyed her home, leaving her with young children and no home to live in. She decided to contact David Mercier & Co. Auctioneer, Durrow, Queens County. Letitia had a clearance sale. All her stock, vehicles and Implements were to be put up for public auction. The auction took place on Friday, the 15th of October 1915.

A New Beginning

Tunduff Park was rebuilt quickly after the fire. A two-storey house, photographed in 1927, replaced the three story one that had been there originally. Unfortunately, there are no images to show of the original house. In the late 1920s, Letitia Dobbs sold the furniture shop in Abbeyleix to John Baggot. Her husband Joseph already died in 1912. Letitia Dobbs née Large died in July 1929.

On June the 28th of 1933, Herbert Conway Dobbs married Margaret Neill Wheeler in St. Peter's Church of Ireland, Belfast, and went on to have two children named George and Peter. George was his only child to have been born in Tunduff Park in 1934, his other son Peter was born in 1940 and became a proud Belfast man. Herbert and his wife Margaret left Abbeyleix when they sold their house and farm at Tunduff Park and moved to Belfast in the late 1930s. Herbert Dobbs was born 1896 and died in 1967, his wife Margaret Dobbs née Wheeler, lived from 1910 to 2012.

When Herbert Dobbs and his wife Margaret left Abbeyleix, it certainly was the end of an era. The family name

Dobbs had been associated with the town of Abbeyleix since 1771. The Dobbs family had created much needed employment for local people that lived here through their various businesses that they operated here.

Tunduff Park 1927.

This picture is of the Dobb's house in Tunduff Park taken in 1927. Herbert took this photo as he had been a keen photographer at the time.

Professions, Merchants, and Traders 1955.

Market Day---Saturday.
Half Holiday---Wednesday.
Population, 1946---522.
Pig Fair---Third Monday of each month.

Auctioneers. John Baggott M.I.A.A.
Bakers. Edward Holohan, EJ Morrissey Main Street. E.
Thornton Ballinakill Road. J. Wilkinson, Main Street.
Banks. Hibernian Bank Ltd. Munster & Leinster Bank Ltd.
Booksellers and Stationers. Brophys, Main Street. EJ
Morrissey, Main Street. P Ryan Main Street.
Bootmakers and Warehouses. Mrs Bergin Leinster House,
Mrs AF Bramley, Conroy Bros, Upper Main Street. W Delaney,
The Square. A Fyffe the Square. J Phelan Stucker Hill. PJ
Walshe Main Street.
Builders and Contractors. Carroll Bros. PH Crennan Main
Street. Denis Kirwan, Main Street.
Bus Service. CIE to Dublin. Thurles, Cashel, and Cork.
Butter and Egg Merchants. JJ Butler, care of EJ Morrissey,
Main Street. Michael Mc Donnell Market Square.
Carpenters. Maurice and John Kelly, Kelly's Cross. M Kelly
Stucker Hill. T Kelly Bluegate. WM Kelly Main Street. T
Mahony & Sons. J Quinn Main Street.
Chemists and Druggists. Armour's Medical Hall, Main Street.
Michael Bree, Main Street.
China and Glass Dealers. John Baggott, Main Street. Brophy's
Main Street. Denis Kirwan, Main Street. Mc Donnell & Sons
the Square. Patrick Ryan Main Street.
Coal Merchants. J Baggott, Main Street. Mrs Bergin, The
Square. S Corrigan, Main Street. JL Lalor Ballinakill Road. PJ
Lalor Main Street. M Mc Donnell Main Street. George Pallin
Oldtown. J Wilkinson, Main Street.
Confectioners. J Quinn Lower Main Street. J Wilkinson, Main
Street.
Corn Merchants. John Baggott, Main Street/. Mc Donnell M
& Sons Market Square.

Cycle Agents. Brambley Bros, Abbeyleix Motor Works, Main Street also agent for Fordson Major Tractors (see advt) H Dooley, Ballinakill Road. Harding's cycle and Motor Works Main Street. Noel O' Connor Lower Main Street.

Dentist. Patrick Fletcher l.R.C.S.I. c/o Wm Delaney Main Street. PP Mc Dermott. George Parkes.

Drapers. F Brambley, Main Street. WM Delaney Main Street. P Fennelly Leinster House. A Fyffe, Market Square. Jack Golden, Stucker Hill. Nolan's, F Phelan, corner house, J Phelan, The Square. PJ Walshe Main Street.

Electrical Dealers. Abbeyleix Motor Works, Main Street. Nicholas Harding, Main Street. Noel O' Connor, Lower Main Street.

Electrical and Radio Engineers. Abbeyleix Motor Works, Main Street. Nicholas Harding, Main Street. Noel O' Connor, Lower Main Street.

Fish Merchants. B Lalor, Temperance Street.

Fruiterers and Green Grocers. Mrs Deegan, Main Street. Brophy's, Main Street. J Quinn Lower Main Street. PJ Lalor, Upper Main Street.

Grocers, Wine & Spirit Merchants. J Armour, Main Street. John Baggott, Main Street. Mrs M Behan, Market Square. J Bergin, Main Street. Mrs Carroll, The Square. James Coady, Market Square. SG Corrigan, Main Street. Denis Kirwan, Main Street. J Lalor Ballinakill Road. PJ Lalor, Stucker Hill. M Mc Donnell, Market Square. Edward Mc Evoy, Main Street. R Mitchell, Main Street. Edward J Morrissey, Main Street. G Pallin, Oldtown. J Phelan the Square. William Phelan, Corner House. Patrick Ryan, Main Street. James Wilkinson, Market Square.

Hairdressers. Beauty Parlour (Miss Phelan). Main Street. E Hinchin, Main Street. Edward Lalor, Ladies and Gents hairdresser, Main Street.

Hardware Merchants and Ironmongers. John Baggott, Main Street. SG Corrigan, Main Street. Denis Kirwan and M Mc Donnell Main Street.

Inn. De Vesci Arms Hotel, Main Street.

Milliners and Dressmakers. Mrs (Marian) Carroll, New Row. Mrs Bergin, Leinster House. Mrs F Brambley, Main Street. W

Delaney, Market Square. Mrs Galbraith, Main Street. Miss A Lalor, Sweetview. Mary Morrissey, The Hotel. Mrs A Ring, Tunduff. PJ Walshe, Main Street.

Motor Engineers and Garages. Abbyleix Motor Works. Nicholas Harding, Main Street. Joe Mc Cabe, Main Street.

Musicians. Mighty Rhythm Kings.

Newsagents. Brophy's, Main Street. Edward J Morrissey, Main Street. Patrick Ryan, Main Street. J Quinn, Lower main Street.

Painters. NP Crennan. Main Street. William Power, Main Street.

Physicians and surgeons. Dr Canty. Dr Mc Donagh. Heath Cottage.

Post Office, W.L. Meredith Main Street.

Saddlers. Patrick Cruite, Ballinakill Road. James Mc Evoy, Ballinakill Road. Charles Ring, Maryborough Road.

Schools. Brigidine Convent Boarding school (girls). Convent National school. North National school for (boys). South National school. Preston school.

Seedsmen. John Baggott, Main Street. Mc Donnell & Co Ltd, The Square. James Wilkinson, The Square.

Solicitors. M Davies, De Vesci Terrace. Fitzsimons & Ryan, Main Street. William T White, Main Street.

Tailors. Fintan Deegan, Balladine Road. Ed Deegan, Main Street.

Tobacconists. John Baggott, Mrs J Bergin, Main Street. Brophy's, James Coady Market Square. R Deegan, Main Street. Denis Kirwan, The Square. J Lalor, Ballinakill Road. PJ Lalor Upper Main Street. Ed Mc Evoy Main Street. Mrs Mooney, Marke Square. R Mitchell, Main Street. EJ Morrissey, Main Street. John O' Reilly Ballinakill Road. George E Pallin, Oldtown. J Quinn, Lower Main Street. Patrick Ryan, Main Street. Edward Thornton, Ballinakill Road. James Wilkinson, Market Square.

Undertakers. M Kelly, Main Street. EJ Morrissey Main Street.

Victuallers. William Gorman, Main Street. Daniel Kennedy, Main Street. Tom Maher & Sons Main Street. J Phelan, The Square.

Veterinary Clinic, Paddy Casserly, Lower Main Street.

Watchmakers and Jewellers. William Comyns, Main Street. Willoughby B & Son Ballinakill Road.
Wine and Spirit Merchants. (See grocers etc). Mrs M Behan, Market Square. Mrs J Bergin, Market Square. Mrs Carroll, The Square. James Coady, Market Square. ED Mc Evoy, Main Street. EJ Morrissey, Main Street. Fintan Phelan, Corner House.

An Tóstal

What was An Tóstal?

Irish meaning - "The Gathering." It was a series of festivals inaugurated in 1953 and continued on a national scale until it died out in 1958. Abbeyleix was no different to lots of other towns throughout the country at the time. They too had their own An Tóstal committee and took part in the celebrations in both 1953 and 1954. The festival aimed to promote Irish culture and attract tourists to Ireland, and Abbeyleix particularly during this period. The organising committees tried to encourage visitors to come and visit our country outside of the normal tourist season.

'The Gathering' is a description attributed by President Seán T O' Kelly in 1953 on the opening of An Tóstal festival with a parade on Dublin's O'Connell Street. The festival had its own flag, which bore the same harp symbol as the official commemorative stamps of the time, designed by Fergus O'Ryan from Limerick. The harp itself was designed by a Dutchman Guss Melai, who used the book of Kells and the Brian Boru harp of Ireland as his inspiration. The initial prompt for An Tóstal came originally from the president of Pan American Airlines who thought Ireland should take inspiration from the 1951 festival of Britain. Presumably, the thought that it might lead to more transatlantic flight bookings didn't cross his mind.

It was particularly aimed at the Irish diaspora in the United States and Board Fáilte Éireann, and the Government realised that it would be a good campaign to promote more visits to Ireland in the off-peak season. It was pitched as a springtime festival and the opening parade was on Easter Sunday, the 5th of April 1953.

Supported By Abbeyleix Businesses

Abbeyleix businesspeople gave their full support, and sponsored various events organised by the An Tóstal committee during the festival. There were parades, sporting events and art festivals among others organised as a means of attracting people to our Town. The committee published two books for the two years that they were involved in, which were in 1953 and 1954. Local authors came out in force to write local stories for the books that were written about the event, and apparently went down very well with the public at large.

They soon found that all the books that they had published were sold out very quickly. An Tóstal largely died out in 1958 throughout the country, with the exception of Drumshambo in Co. Leitrim where it continued until 2019. Two events that have happened and continued because of this festival were the beginning of the Tidy Towns competition, and the Rose of Tralee.

Parades and Marches
The older generation in Abbeyleix town loved to take part in Parades and Marches and did so in 1953. They performed at various events at the An Tóstal festival as seen in the photograph named 'A Political meeting.' Fint Coffey was the last surviving member of that group until he passed away on the 16 November 2018. Fint was also a member of the Abbeyleix pipe band.

Three members of the Abbeyleix Pipe Band are still alive today - Paul Fennelly from Thornberry, Tommy Gorman, and Andy McEvoy. They entertained the local people for years at numerous parades and events. Paul can be seen sitting beside Joe Clooney that lived in Balladine. Séamus Clooney, a son of

Joe, entertained George Clooney when he visited his cousins in Abbeyleix in Easter 2019.

When you sit, ponder, and reflect back on your life, living and growing up in Abbeyleix, why not document a story about a memory that stands out in your mind, so that they can be passed on to the generations to follow? When you get to a stage in your life where you like to look back on the life you have lived, it's lovely to recall memories of people that you knew and the stories that they told.

Preserve the Past for the future.

The Brigidine School

Abbeyleix 1996
On Friday the 12th of July 1996, the end of an era in the history
of Abbeyleix was marked at a ceremony. As the school year
ended in June 1996, the Brigidine Sisters and the Patrician
Brothers, who had contributed so much to the educational and
cultural development of the community for over 200 years,
formally ended their association with schooling in Abbeyleix.
Under the guidance of Fr. Patrick Keogh PP. Abbeyleix, the past
pupils and friends of the Brigidine Sisters and the Patrician
Brothers met regularly to plan the ceremonies.

    The evening started with con-celebrated Mass at 7.30
pm on the Friday evening the 12th of July, in the Church of the
most Holy Rosary Abbeyleix. The chief celebrant was the
Bishop of Kildare and Leighlin, Dr. Laurence Ryan, joined by
the priests of the parish, and other priests that were ordained in
Abbeyleix, or served as curates in the parish. The Brigidine
Nuns and Patrician Brothers who taught in the schools in
Abbeyleix were invited back, and they were the VIPs for the
night.

    After the Mass, the activities continued in the
Abbeyleix Heritage House, which was once the old North
School. This was the first function that was held in the Heritage
House. It enabled the community to see the transformation

Abbeyleix Heritage company had achieved. The committee had commissioned special stone plaques to be erected at the Heritage House as a tribute to the Brigidines and the Patricians. All the past pupils of the Brigidine, national and secondary schools were invited to attend on the night.

Where It All Began

The Brigidine story began on the 1st of February 1807 when Daniel Delaney, Bishop of Kildare and Leighlin, invited six nuns to form a religious community in Tullow, Co Carlow. He named them the sisters of Saint Bridget, after the great 5th century Saint of Kildare.

Born in 1747, Daniel Delaney was the first of two sons of an affluent farming family on the Castlecoote Estate. His father Daniel and younger brother John died when Daniel was still young. The Brigidine Convent national and secondary schools were established in Abbeyleix in 1842 and the first residential student, a Miss Lynch from Loughshinney, situated between Rush and Skerries in Co. Dublin, was first to be admitted in 1844. The first confirmation class was prepared by the Brigidines in 1845. The school began to advertise for boarders in 1852 and by 1870 the numbers increased to 60. From here, the Brigidine Convent expanded, and education of a very high standard was provided.

The Brigidine Sisters felt that a student should be physically and emotionally healthy and stay focused to perform well in their academics. Including sports activities in the curriculum could help them to achieve this to a great extent, and that's what they did. Prior to Monday the 31st of December 1962 when the railway station closed and a hard winter with snow everywhere befell Abbeyleix, there are still some local people living in the town that can remember some of the boarders returning to the convent from Dublin on a Sunday evening. The boarders were collected at the station by one of the work men with the convents horse and cart.

Orla Remembers

Orla, a boarder of the Abbeyleix convent from September 1979 to June 1984, recalls her memories from her time there. Many girls came to the boarding school in Abbeyleix from different parts of the country, simply because their mothers had done so before them.

The head of the boarding school at the time was mother superior Sr Breda Ryan, and principal was Sr Phil O' Shea. Sr Una and Sr Elizabeth taught home economics and Sr Teresa taught Geography. Most of the teachers were lay teachers at that time. Orla had some great teachers. Sr Teresa for Geography, Mrs Quinn for Science, Biology and Chemistry.

"She was scary but brilliant," Orla believed Mrs Quinn was Bobby Sands sister as "there was a story going around at the time that a helicopter had landed near the convent and took her to the North when her brother was on hunger strike."

Orla's not certain of this but it was a strong rumour there at that time! Malachy Fogarty was the most patient maths teacher in history, Orla recalls. Mrs Kala Donoghue was the English teacher in sixth year, although she was strict all the girls respected her. When Mrs Donoghue got sick and had to leave the school, all the girls in her class really missed her. These girls were the last class to have been taught by Mrs Kala Donoghue.

There were approximately 74 boarders in the convent at that time. During her time in the convent, Orla recalls that she particularly remembers three musicals. The first musical told the story of a touring flea circus. It was an internationally acclaimed musical and was very funny. "The Donkey in particular played by Marion Kenny was a touch of class."

The classic *Wizard of Oz* was produced in 1982 by Miss Sandra Lynch. Miss Majella Murphy was the music teacher at the time. The lead role of Dorothy, played by Rhonwyn Hayes, was a Dublin girl. Orla always thought that

Rhonwyn would end up on the stage in later life. The Brigidine production of *Scrooge* in 1984 based on Dicken's *A Christmas Carol* was also produced by Sandra Lynch and the music by Majella Murphy. This was their second success.

The convent school had a successful senior basketball team. Orla loved being let out of study to watch the matches. The school also had very successful volleyball teams during her time there. During the early summer months, there was normal athletics races run around the green area below the tennis courts. She remembers both the long and the high jump also. They played tennis, but it was never played competitively to the best of her knowledge.

In first year, Orla recalls as a boarder having retreat nights, which she enjoyed as there was always lovely songs to listen to. Therese English gave a great rendition of 'Bright Eyes'. She doesn't think that this event continued through the years. A tradition that also died out after her first year in boarding school was the first-year students putting on a talent show for the boarding school. A few senior students helped to put a show together, which was enjoyed by all. In Orla's first year, her piece was to act out a popular advertisement on television at the time - 'The Guinness 30 seconds of Darkness'. These plays helped to build confidence and prepare the students for the second year in boarding school.

Another tradition that had finished by the time that Orla reached 6th year, was the Ballyfin College dance where only the 6th year boarders attended. For the next term, the Ballyfin College boys would come to Abbeyleix for a dance. Great excitement spread amongst boarders as the older girls got ready for the dance. As boarders, they loved when a feast day fell on a Thursday, as there was no school that day, so they got to watch *Top of the Pops*. They got to see the 6pm news each evening before study began.

Between September 1979 and June 1984, there were three school tours abroad. In London, they visited Madame Tussauds, watched the West End Show *Evita*, and visited other sites including Trafalgar Square and Buckingham Palace. A trip to France by boat with gale force winds blowing resulted in many girls becoming extremely sick on their way home. The final trip was to Germany where they were due to go on a boat trip on the Rhine, but it was flooded and too dangerous, so they travelled by road on the same route by bus. They flew into Düsseldorf, then travelled to Koblenz, a city on the banks of the Rhine, and finally Frankfurt. Travelling to Germany was Orla's first time on an aeroplane, which was an experience in itself.

The Brigidine Sisters were quite self-sufficient in many ways as they had their own farm, where they grew all their own potatoes and vegetables, and hay for the horses, among lots of other things. The Sisters did all their own baking. They baked buns, cakes, and bread, and when they were baked the sister in charge would place the freshly baked bread on a tray and leave them outside the kitchen door to cool down. Orla recalls a local woman who relieved the nuns of one or two loafs when they weren't watching. The young girl at the time was not a boarder. Although the convent was enclosed by a high wall on the North and the East side, a steel gate with a wicket gate in the centre of it allowed the workmen to enter and leave the convent while on their way in and out to the farm. The gardener also used the same little gate entrance. This girl, who shall remain nameless, noticed how the workmen entered and left the convent, while she often took a short cut through the graveyard from her home, while on her way to the town. The young girl enjoyed visiting the convent orchard and collecting a few sweet apples as well. The young girl was never caught doing so, although she didn't do it too often!

The Magazine

The publication of a 1990 yearbook by the students of the Brigidine Convent signified the end of an era. It marked the closing of the school and the setting up of the new Community School in Ballinakill. 10 years had passed since a similar magazine was published and the sixth years felt that this was the year to commemorate their school which enjoyed an excellent reputation for over 150 years.

Pupils, teachers, and the chairwoman of the parents committee contributed to the magazine. Caroline Mc Closkey and Yvonne Reilly traced the history of the convent from 1842 up to 1990 and wrote about it in the magazine. Sr Finbar

Richardson wrote about her experience as she attended the Brigidine Convent as a pupil when she was only 11 years old and became a Brigidine Sister herself. Maura Whelan and Sinead Lacey wrote a piece on the musicals staged in the school over the years. Volleyball news was written by Mary Clare Rohan, senior team captain who recalls the long tradition of the sport in the school and outlines the recent big successes there.

Monica Reilly, who later graduated with a Master's Degree in Education from Eastern Kentucky University in December of that year, remembers being told, "Miss Reilly you'll never be good for anything, only running and gallivanting around a golf course."

Monica recalled that her athletic abilities and her excellent secondary school education opened many doors for her. Catherine Reilly, Monica's sister, was also a gifted sports lady, especially at golf, she too attended the Brigidine convent. Mary Bridget Maher from Abbeyleix outlines that her time as a pupil there coincided with the last two years of World War ll.

The award-winning fashion designer Louise Kennedy was in the 'Class of 78.' Patricia Mc Cabe from Abbeyleix, Brenda O' Dwyer, and Mary Kavanagh organised a reunion for the leaving Cert Class of 1978, which was held in the Killeshin Hotel in Portlaoise. It was held on the 22nd of September 1990. As many as 35 of the girls attended the reunion, where they all enjoyed catching up on old times. One of the girls had travelled from Bahrain, and two from England to attend the reunion.

The End was in Sight

In 1987, the last Leaving Certificate exams were sat in the Convent. The school closed in 1990. The Brigidine nuns continued with their commitment to educate in the new national school. The new school, as it was called, was Scoil Mhuire, built in 1983. The Sisters continued their involvement in education up until June 1996, both in Heywood Community School and Scoil Mhuire before ending their 200 plus years of educating in Abbeyleix.

The Patrician Brothers

The Patrician Brothers were founded in 1808 in Tullow, Co Carlow, by Bishop Daniel Delaney. The Brotherhood was founded on the feast of the Purification of the Blessed Virgin Mary, one year after he had founded the Brigidine Sisters. Bishop Daniel Delaney's favourite armchair can be viewed in the Heritage house Museum in Abbeyleix.

The story of the Patrician Brothers in the field of education in Abbeyleix commenced on July the 1st in 1933 and ended on the 30th of June 1996. An ironic feature of the Patrician Brothers involvement in schooling in Abbeyleix is that they were invited and welcomed to the town by Fr. John Breen, PP in 1933 and on the 12th of July 1996 his grand-nephew Fr. Patrick Keogh PP oversaw their departure from the field of education in Abbeyleix. The Patrician Brothers school opened in July 1933 by Brother Cronin Commins the principal and Brother Luke Moroney his assistant. The Patrician Brothers were in place in the North school on the 1st of July 1933.

The first children sent to the school were boys aged seven and eight years old from the convent infants' school. Some of the names of the first children to attend the Patrician Brothers who may still be familiar with the people of Abbeyleix were - Noel Crennan, Paddy Kelly, Billy O Gorman, Jackie Bergin, Seamus Johnson, John Hill, Joe Johnson, Jack Clooney, Michael Dunphy, Billy Bonham, Lorcan O Toole, Bill Viney, Kevin Hogan, Stephen Cummins, Joe Dooley, Sean Lalor, Paddy Mc Evoy, and Jim Quinn.

The Patrician Brothers were responsible for training the Abbeyleix juvenile hurling teams. Numerous county championships were won under their leadership. The Brothers also took a keen interest in music, where they went on to form the Patrician Brothers school accordion band. The Brothers were proud of the school choir that they formed and had entered them in singing competitions, especially in those early years. I can remember staying behind after school hours on at least one occasion to practice for the school play that the brothers were keen to have performed on a public stage which was in this case the old C.Y.M.S. hall in the town. The school's accordion band would perform and provide the musical entertainment for the audience at the show.

Michael Mills the former ombudsman and journalist, Paddy Lalor a former TD, Government minister and MEP were both pupils of the Patrician Brothers school back in the day. These schools are now long gone, and lots has changed, but they are still remembered, especially for their impact on the town of Abbeyleix and its students.

Christy Phelan

In 1996, the passing of an Abbeyleix legend happened. Christy Phelan passed away on Thursday the 6th of June 1996. Born in 1926, he grew up living in a house at the top of the town known as the Tiles. Christy was a member of a long-established and highly respected Abbeyleix family. He worked in the hardware business, first with Paddy Mc Donald, then with Sam Pratt, and finally with Ken Murphy. For 38 years he was a member of the Abbeyleix Fire Brigade, serving as an officer and then as a sub officer for the remainder of his service. He was promoted to Station Officer in 1975 before retiring in 1988

Christy helped to establish the local Credit Union and was associated with the local GAA and the C.Y.M.S. Indeed, he was very much interested in all sports. He also took a keen interest in the welfare of all other clubs and organisations in the area as well. Christy was a religious man. He planned to make his second pilgrimage to Lourdes organised by Paddy Mulhall

and Malachy Mc Evoy on Sunday the 23rd of June that same year, the rate was £360 per person. Sadly, it was not to be.

Christy passed away rather unexpectedly at his home in Balladine on June 6th. He was as honest in all his dealing, as the day was long. He was in a mould of his own and is irreplaceable in so many ways. A man of high ideals, he commanded utmost respect wherever he

went and most especially in his hometown that he served so well over many decades.

Christy was a legend in his own lifetime, and his passing was a sore loss to Abbeyleix, the town he loved so well. I believe that the people of this town, and indeed everyone who knew him, should take a moment to reflect on what a wonderful man Christy Phelan was.

Gifted Correspondent

Christy was a correspondent with the Leinster Express for forty years. When you think about the work that he had to do, in order to get his news articles into the paper on a weekly basis, it doesn't bear thinking about. It's unbelievable given the constraints he was under. Without the use of a car, mobile phone, email, zoom calls, fax machines (which were only invented in 1964, but only became popular with consumers in the 1980s), and all the technology that we have today, he had to work 6 days a week. A half day on a Wednesday was the short break he had, with Sunday being the only day of the week that he had to himself. Christy had to source the news article first, research them and write the article. He would then deliver them to the Leinster Express office in Portlaoise before the deadline. His way of delivering the articles involved calling on the services of our photographer James G Carroll.

At that time James was completing his secondary education in Portlaoise which happened to be opposite the Leinster Express office. His job was to collect the news articles from Christy's home and deliver them to the office while on a break from his class, and this worked for as long as James attended this school.

The 1950's

Christy began writing for the Leinster Express in the mid-1950s. He took over from Paddy Lalor who of course went on to become a Minister and an MEP.

When Christy took over writing for the paper, his life was devoted to keeping Abbeyleix in the forefront, and the success of his efforts were fully reflected in the pages of the Leinster Express every week. As a weekly correspondent for the paper, he far exceeded the call of duty. He was prolific in his writings, and he ensured that nothing of note from his area was left unreported. His love for the town and his enthusiasm in raising awareness in particular organisations or functions sometimes caused ripples in certain areas. If that was the case, it was all done in the interest of rousing a positive response.

Christy was a man that shot straight from the hip. Everyone knew where he stood on any particular subject. He was as meticulous as he was fearless and rarely could anyone point a finger at his reports for even the slightest inaccuracy. He went to extraordinary lengths to get the full and rounded story.

Sad Loss

Christy's passing caused widespread shock and disbelief at the time because he passed away so unexpectedly. You always felt that you were his friend. A colleague of his in the fire service Paddy Kelly had passed away six days earlier only adding to the sadness and sorrow that the people of our town felt. The biggest loss of all was felt of course by his wife Agnes, and his devoted family to whom sincere sympathy was extended.

A huge crowd attended the Requiem Mass for his funeral which attested to the respect in which he was regarded. Rev. Patrick Finnerty CC. received the remains in the Church. Fire Brigade officers from various parts of the county formed a guard of honour. Principal celebrants of the Requiem Mass were Rev Patrick Keogh, PP. of Abbeyleix assisted by Rev. Finnerty, Rev. Eddie Lalor of Kenya; and Rev. John O' Brien, CC. of Mountrath. At the Mass Fr. Keogh and Eddie Thornton, on behalf of the Credit Union, paid tribute to Christy. In the congregation were Teddy Fennelly, Managing Editor, and John Whelan, News Editor, representing the Leinster Express.

The 25th Anniversary

2021 was the 25th anniversary of Christy's passing, A man like Christy Phelan deserves to be remembered by the people of Abbeyleix, a man that you can truly say loved his hometown.

I would just like to say to Christy Phelan's family that we the people of Abbeyleix, his friends and indeed everyone that knew him, haven't forgotten him and he is in our thoughts and prayers at this time. Our sympathies are still with Christy's family, his wife Agnes, son Martin, daughters Mary, Rita, June, Geraldine, and Fionnuala, daughter-in law Helen, grandsons James and David, nephews, nieces, relatives, and friends. Ar dheist Dé go raibh a h'anam dílis.

ABBEYLEIX FIRE BRIGADE 1960.
Back Row L/R Hugh O'Connor. Patrick Hill. Martin Dunne. Billy Whelan. Patrick McHugh. Joe McGrath.
Front Row L/R John Gorman. Christy Phelan. Timothy Bonham.

Cluain Chaoin - The Beautiful Meadow

Clonkeen, also known locally as Clonking, is a small townland situated some three kilometres south of the Heritage Town of Abbeyleix. Just east of the main Dublin to Cork Road, it has been a centre of habitation for many centuries. Clonkeen derives its name from the Irish 'Cluain Chaoin' meaning the Beautiful or Quiet Meadow.

Protected by the gentle slopes of the foothills of the Sliabh Margy mountains and overlooking the rolling plains of Magh Lacha, Clonkeen has, for most of its history, been an island of tranquillity and peaceful retreat. Traces of a pre-historic Rath can still be seen on the high ground to the South of the townland which would indicate that among the first inhabitants of this region where the Tuathe Dé Dannan. The Rath builders came to Ireland from the eastern Mediterranean some 4000 years ago. The Tuathe Dé Dannan civilisation lasted in Ireland for over a thousand years. How long the Clonkeen settlement existed is not known, but while they were here, there must have been many occasions when they enjoyed the marvellous view from their Rath as the sun set across the vast plain of Magh Lacha, the Plain of the Lakes, stretching as far as the eye can see to the southwest.

Clonkeen became a place of more permanent habitations around 600 AD, when historians believe a monastic foundation was established in the centre of the townland. Some archaeologists are of the opinion that the ruins of the old Church, still to be seen in Clonkeen, date from that original foundation. Sir Charles Coote refers to the foundation of an Abbey in the area in the year 600 AD, and it is possible that this was the Monastery in Clonkeen. The major religious establishments at Aghaboe and Cloneagh were founded during the same period of time, and some have surmised that Clonkeen Monastery may well have been set up as a place of rest and retreat for the monks and religious of the more prestigious foundations.

The ancient historian Colgan, says that St. Fintan, the renowned founder of the famous Monastery at Clonenagh, was born in Clonkeen and through the years there are many instances of saintly Abbots of Clonenagh and Aghaboe retiring to Clonkeen or Dysart for periods of retreat and spiritual refreshment. Located off the beaten track, Clonkeen lies near the river Nore, with its view of the plain of Magh Lacha being admirably suited for that purpose.

Archdall records several Abbots and Bishops in Clonkeen over the years. Anchorite, St. Fintan, who died in the Monastery in 860 AD whose feast day is on the 7th of February. Lucell, the Bright One, has a feast day on the 6th of October. Arvinius, also known as Aaron, has a festival on the 1st of August. Dimocus or Modicomus, has a feast day on the 8th of December, and Daghaues has a feast day on the 18th of August. Another St. Fintan, a holy priest of the Abbey of Clonkeen, was celebrated on the 11th of May.

There is another district named Clonkeen, or Clonehene, very close to the site of the Abbey of Clonenagh. Some confusion is inevitable as to which Clonkeen ancient historians were referring to. It is possible that some of the events and saints mentioned above referred to the Clonkeen of the Clonenagh district, but it is unlikely that there was a separate Abbey in Clonkeen so close to Clonenagh Abbey. It would seem more likely that Bishops and Abbots of Clonkeen were of the monastic foundation at Clonkeen near Abbeyleix.

In these early years of Christianity, the Monasteries and Abbeys tended to become the centres of civilisation. There were no towns and cities as such, until groups of dwellings developed around the Abbeys forming villages and communities. Clonkeen was no exception. As an extensive community lived in the locality, it remained the main centre of population in the region for over 500 years. The local Abbot and monks served the religious needs of the community. Many of whom were employed by the Monastery in the provision of food from farming and hunting.

The pre-Norman parish of Clonkeen stretched from Loughill up to the present town of Abbeyleix in the north, and from Watercastle in the west over to and Ballinakill in the east. Clonkeen Church appears on an early map of the region, published in 1563. It is marked as *Clocuiane*, and is linked with the Cistercian Abbey of Leix, founded in 1183, under the regional name of *Franamanagh*, which translates as the Land of the Monks. Certainly, the Parish of Clonkeen must have been of some considerable significance as soon after the Anglo-Norman invasion it became the object of a long and bitter dispute between the Bishop of Leighlin in whose diocese it was situated, and the Prior of Great Connall in Kildare.

History is obscure as to the nature of the claims of the various parties in the dispute, but it was eventually settled when the parish of Clonkeen became appropriate in the Prior of Great Connall, and the bishop Leighlin and his successors were to be paid a sum of 30 marks, a considerable amount of money in those days, each year in perpetuity. Very little is on record of the pastors or clergymen who ministered to the people of Clonkeen in these pre-Reformation years. Two received passing mention in various records - Canon Geoffreay O' Byrne in 1482, and Canon James O' Curryn in 1506. Later, Clonkeen townland became part of the lands of the Abbey of Leix, and the rectory of Loughill were amalgamated and became the Rectory of Clonkeen. It remained so for the next two centuries.

By 1552, all Monastic buildings and lands in the area had been granted to the Butlers, Earls of Ormond, and remained in their possession for nearly eighty years although under frequent attack from the O' Moores and O' Carrolls. In the Protestant tradition, the first recorded Vicar of Clonkeen in 1616 was Thomas Smith, M.A., who was Minister and Preacher, at £15 per annum and a residence. Where his residence was, is not recorded. It is known that the church of Clonkeen was in good repair at that time and contained many books and other religious artefacts. Another Vicar of these times was Thomas Bingham who was installed as Vicar in 1641. Thomas was the unfortunate victim of one of the few instances of the tragedy of war sweeping across Clonkeen.

According to a deposition given by his wife Ann in 1643, he was killed by the rebels. His head was decapitated and carried to the Ormonds in Kilkenny. It is perhaps not surprising that the next Vicar of Clonkeen on record, Ithel Walker, was not installed until 1661. In 1637, however the Butler lands around Abbeyleix, including Clonkeen, reverted to the crown. These same lands were granted by King Charles II to Sir Edward Massey in 1663 and were subsequently sold by his son in 1675 to Denny Muschamp, one-time Munster's Master General of the crown forces in Ireland. When Muschamp's daughter, Mary, married Sir Thomas Vesey, Baronet, in 1699, Denny Muschamp gave them Abbeyleix Manor and Estates as a wedding gift.

The Vesci family, later to become de Vesci, became introduced to the area. By 1718, Sir Thomas de Vesci had become Bishop of Ossory and purchased the fee simple of all the estates, and the property including Clonkeen was to remain in the de Vesci family for over two hundred years. In 1730, a new Vicar was installed in Clonkeen, by the name of Muschamp Vesci, possibly the son of Sir Thomas and Mary Vesci. It is of interest to note that he was installed 'Vicar of Clonkeen alias Abbeyleix', which would indicate the beginning of the change whereby the village of Abbeyleix began to take precedence over Clonkeen. The religious significance of the Parish of Clonkeen in both the Protestant and the Catholic traditions seemed to have diminished somewhat as the years progressed, although there is a tradition of a conference of seven Catholic Bishops taking place here in the 18th century.

This was the era of the Penal Laws which were designed to suppress Irish Catholicism. The relative remoteness of Clonkeen made it a likely venue for such a conference. This region was still largely a mixture of dense forest and marshy bogs and was very much off the beaten track. One commentator of the time described conditions by stating that, "the forest primeval holds sway, nothing but a wilderness of trackless woods of hazel and sally and treacherous bogs." Up to 1730, masses were celebrated in what is still known as the Mass field, on the western borders of the old parish of Clonkeen at Kenny's gravel pit.

In 1704, under the act of Registration of Popish Clergy, one of the priests who registered in Maryborough, now Portlaoise, was Fr. Connell Moore, Parish Priest of Clonkeen. Despite the Penal Laws, Fr. Moore had many successors. One of whom is mentioned in the 'Returns on Popery' by the Protestant Bishop of Leighlin and Ferns in 1731. In his report on the Clonkeen region he states that "there is but one Mass house in Clonkeen, a boarded covering in the fields, and one priest, William Keating, P.P., and one schoolmaster."

Over 200 hundred years ago, as the new town of Abbeyleix developed, a new Catholic Church was built in the town and Clonkeen became incorporated into the new Parish of Abbeyleix. In the 1920's, Clonkeen became part of the Parish of Ballinakill in the Catholic tradition, as is still the case today. At what time the Church fell into disuse and disrepair is not

known, but from the above report it is unlikely that it was in use in 1731 by either tradition. Legend has it that the roof of the Church was dismantled in the 1600s by the Earl of Ormond, and its lead removed to roof an extension to Kilkenny Castle. The Parish Church of Clonkeen consisted of a nave (central part of a church) and a chancel (space around the altar). The walls of the nave, which according to archaeologists may be part of the original foundation, are essentially preserved although almost completely covered with ivy. The chancel, which was a later addition probably around the year 1400, with an ogee-headed east window, meaning a continuous S-shaped curve, collapsed from its foundations almost 120 years ago. There is no connecting opening between the nave and the chancel. The surrounding graveyard contains gravestones with dates spanning the last two hundred years. The present-day enclosing wall was built about one hundred and twenty-five years ago by Patrick and Edward Waters, father and son stonemasons from Castlemarket, Co. Kilkenny, situated close to Ballinakill in Co. Laois. Previously, the graveyard was three times larger than it is now. A previous landowner reported that when he attempted to plough the field adjacent to the graveyard in Clonkeen, he began to unearth human bones. Immediately, he ceased work and declared he would never unearth the soil in that field again. The present owner of this farm has made the same decision never to unearth the soil in this field. Hopefully, in the near future, a scientific survey can be carried out to determine the extent of this burial ground. A process of cleaning and restoration of the Church and its grounds is planned for the near future. A Mass has already been said at this site some 700 years since its last ceremony. Fr. Paddy Byrne, PP of Abbeyleix celebrated a Mass on the 14th of September 2022, where many people attended.

Despite wars and famines, the population of the townland of Clonkeen was considerable during the 18th and 19th centuries. In 1815, over a period of months, the southern end of what is now the Killamuck bog slipped down from the hill to the west, slowly enveloped many of the mud and stone houses of the northern part of Clonkeen. It is intended that part of this southern end of the bog should be preserved, both as an example of bogland flora and fauna, and because of what future scientific investigation might discover underneath the surface. One section of the bog is known as 'Wild Lough', and the woodland on the hill on the eastern edge of Clonkeen is known as 'Lacha Wood', which may be interpreted as the Elm Wood or perhaps the Wood of the Lake. It may be that at one time this was a lake, particularly as there is no evidence of elms being planted in the area.

The 1841 census of Ireland registered 44 dwellings in Clonkeen, housing almost 300 people. In the mid-1840s, the Great Famine had a dramatic effect on the area, but even so, up to the beginning of the 20th century there was always a hearthstone for every acre in Clonkeen, with a flax factory situated on the hills to the east providing some employment for the area. Not too far from the old Church, the ruins of the old schoolhouse can be seen, and some of the older families of the area talk of their grandparents going to school there at a cost of two old pence, 1p or 1 cent a day. During the first half of this century, the population of Clonkeen dwindled somewhat mainly as a result of emigration over the years.

During the last two centuries burials in both Catholic and Protestant traditions have taken place in Clonkeen. The last internment in the graveyard took place in 1979, a man by the name of John Parkinson from Clonking. Recent times has seen the return of some members of older families to establish new homes in the region. Over the centuries, the aristocracy, both religious and secular sought out and enjoyed the serenity and solitude of the Clonkeen environment and the health-given 'bog

air.' Clonkeen, to this day, still retains its quiet beauty, its charm, and gentle tranquillity. In many ways it still is Cluain Chaoin, the Quite and Beautiful Meadow. *Pictured: Grainne Fennelly*

Dan O' Sullivan

Dan O' Sullivan, who was he?

From the turn of the century up to the arrival of the Patrician
Brothers in Abbeyleix in 1933, the Abbeyleix Boys' National
School at Stucker Hill had been taken in charge by a lay
teacher, Dan O'Sullivan. Mr Dan O' Sullivan was a Cork man
with teaching methods that might not always have been in
complete line with the Department of Education's directives.
Knowing that second level education was out of the reach for
the vast majority of his pupils, he stretched the curriculum to
give them the broadest education possible, and in a way that
made an indelible mark. Indeed, over the years, many of the
boys went on from his sixth and seventh classes to successful
careers in various fields at home and overseas. Although he is
long gone to his eternal reward, Danny, as he was familiarly
known, is still well remembered in Abbeyleix in 1984.

I Remember My School Days in the 1920s

The following is an account of an Abbeyleix senior citizens
memories of his schooldays, written in the form of a poem
about his time at the National Boys' School in Stucker Hill in
Abbeyleix, situated at the top of the town. It was also known as
the North Monastery school. Lal Deegan compiled this poem on
reflection of the time he spent going to that school in the early
1920s. Written in 1984, the poem is about a teacher that he had
great time for whose name was Mr Dan O' Sullivan.

*There are no days like your young days and those days were
better still.*
For us who got our schooling above on Stucker Hill.
The master was a Corkman, O' Sullivan was his name.
But we all called him "Danny" and widespread was his fame.
He taught us all there was to know, as well as any college.
*Prepared us all for the great big world, with a wealth of general
knowledge.*

He showed us how to read and write; no word we could not spell.
And we knew our tables backwards, and arithmetic as well.
In algebra he taught us how to add and multiply
He proved how problems could be solved with letters x and y.
On days when we'd conduct ourselves with signs of some decorum.
He'd tell us Euclid proved his theorem, Pons Asinorum.

Bhí Gaeilge go leor aige; he spoke with true Cork blas.
And for history and for folklore he was never at a loss.
He taught the best of poetry, adding "Pinch and Coach O' Leary."
And he'd read the paper – every line – when Cork beat Tipperary.
He told what nouns and pronouns were and taught us how to parse.
And he never slapped us on the hands - just a wallop on the arse.

When he got us out around Europe's map, was the time that we liked best.
He told us tales of places from, Ballyroan to Budapest.
He'd show Italy kicking Sicily in the Mediterranean Sea.
He'd take us all through Spain and France and into Germany.
We'd travel all through Russia then to the Holy Land.
And we'd finish on Mount Ararat where Noah's Ark did stand.

Before the yearly religious test 'twas "Study" all day long.
We learned each chapter inside out and never answered wrong.
We read the holy Gospels, too – Mark, Matthew, Luke, and John.
We had the parables off by heart, Samaritan, Prodigal Son.
But even teaching bible, "Danny" uttered rare old spakes.
He called a brood of vipers, "a clutch of clucking snakes".

Lads walked to school in those old days – from as far away as Kyle.

There were hard 'chaws' down from Ballydine and bright boys
from Rathmoyle.
And the Killamuck boys from the bog were always coming late.
They would creep like snails along the street and run for the
school's gate.
But they weren't codding "Danny", He knew their every trick.
He would wait inside the door and mark them present with his
stick.

God forgive us "Danny", sure we didn't treat you fair.
We made jokes about your cranium and its scarcity of hair.
We got up to every devilment when you went outside the door.
We put every sally stick you had through the knotholes in the
floor.
But when Gabriel blows, you'll call the roll inside the Pearly
gates.
We'll be on time, the 'cherubs', you once tried to educate.

The De Vesci Family & Florence Nightingale

Lady Emma de Vesci

The people of Abbeyleix are very much aware of the presence of the de Vesci family living in this area dating back to the 1700s right up to the present day, where Thomas Vesey, 7th Viscount de Vesci (pictured) and 8th Baron of Knapton, still lives.

In 1839, Lady Emma (1819-1884) married Thomas the future Lord de Vesci (1803-1875). Emma was somewhat of an unsung hero of her time. As many of you may be aware, Emma saved the lives of many hundreds of people that lived in the Abbeyleix area during the time of the famine which began in 1845.

Emma set up soup kitchens in the town that were much appreciated and indeed availed of by the hundreds of poor and destitute people that lived in our town. Emma and her husband Thomas did everything they could to lessen the suffering of the people from this town and the surrounding areas. Of course, thousands of Irish people were badly affected and suffered tremendously as a result of the famine which spread throughout the whole country at the time.

Lady Emma was involved and played her part in helping the relatively new town of Abbeyleix to prosper and grow during her time living here. She organised a major renovation of the modern Church of Ireland in the 1860s. The work resulted in the dismantling of the older Church except for the belltower and spire. It also involved the rebuilding of the structure under the direction of architect Mr. Thomas Wyatt. The present-day Heritage House in Abbeyleix was the original North School constructed under the guidance of Lady Emma de Vesci. The school was completed in 1885 almost one year after her death. The purpose of this school was to provide primary education for the Catholic boys of the town and surrounding areas. Lady Emma also designed the memorial Gothic fountain at the lower end of the town of Abbeyleix in remembrance of her late husband. She was also an entrepreneurial woman, co- founding the Abbeyleix Baby Linen Society in 1845 which supplied affordable children's clothes to women of the area.

Florence Nightingale

Florence Nightingale was an English social reformer, statistician, and the founder of modern nursing. Nightingale came to prominence while serving as a manager and trainer of nurses during the Crimean war, in which she organised care for the wounded soldiers at Constantinople. Florence Nightingale also became known as the 'Lady with the Lamp' during the war that lasted from 1853-1856.

The Crimean war was a military conflict fought between Russia and an alliance of France, the Ottoman Empire, the United Kingdom, and Piedmont -Sardinia. The cause of the war involved the rights of Christian minorities in Palestine, which was part of the Ottoman Empire. This war was also intended to limit Russian expansion into Europe. Russia eventually lost in 1856. In 1907, Florence was the first woman to receive the Order of Merit, Britain's highest civilian decoration.

While stationed in Crimea, Florence Nightingale developed the 'Crimean fever' - a bacterial infection now known as brucellosis - and never recovered. Approximately four years after she returned from the war she became mostly bed-bound and remained so for the rest of her life. Named after her birth place, Florence Nightingale was born in May 1820. She died in Mayfair London in August 1910. In her lifetime, she was awarded the Royal Red Cross (1883), Lady of Grace of the Order of St John (1904) and the Order of Merit in (1907).

The Link

Lady Emma de Vesci's brother, Lord Sidney Herbert of Lea, was a ground-breaking progressive philanthropist and a British politician. He was a great supporter of Florence Nightingale. Without the influence of Lord Herbert, The Lady of the Lamp would never have obtained sufficient funds or British Government support to start her first hospital in the Crimean war. In 1884, under the authorization of Sidney Herbert, the secretary of war, Florence Nightingale brought a team of 38 volunteer nurses to care for the British soldiers fighting in the Crimean War.

In 1858, for her contributions to army and hospital statistics Nightingale became the first woman elected to be a fellow of the Royal Statistical Society.

In 1860, the Nightingale Training School and Home for Nurses, based at St Thomas's Hospital in London, opened with 10 students. It was financed by the Nightingale Fund, a fund of public contributions set up during Nightingale's time in Crimea and had raised a total of £50,000. It was based around two principles. Firstly, that the nurses should have practical training in hospitals specially organised for that purpose. Secondly, the nurses should live in a home fit to form a moral life and discipline. Due to the foundation of this school, Nightingale achieved the transformation of nursing from its disreputable past into a responsible and respectable career for women. Nightingale responded to the British war office's request for advice on army medical care in Canada and also consulted the United States government on army health during the American Civil war.

The quality and professionalism of nursing that we are all very much accustomed to now, can be traced back to the professional teaching methods of Florence Nightingale. From our own hospital here in Abbeyleix to hospitals across our county and country. Nightingale designed a nursing management structure known as the 'Nightingale Method', where it was possible for women to rise through the profession from Probationer to Superintendent.

Another Important Abbeyleix Connection

Doctor William Boxwell was not only a physician but was also a teaching Surgeon that practised here in Abbeyleix for twenty-five years prior to his death. His practice in the town also included the doctor in charge of the Workhouse Infirmary that opened in June 1842 which housed the poor and destitute people from this area. Boxwell lived in Woodville House in town where the Casserly family now live.

Born into a Church of Ireland family in Wexford on May the 10th 1796, Boxwell moved to Abbeyleix as a Police Surgeon around 1822 where he lived with his wife, Sarah. They had eight children, two of which died young. Doctor Boxwell came from a very prominent family in Wexford. His father John came from an old Cromwellian family and was educated in Trinity. John was touched by the plight of the poor people in his locality in Wexford and took part in the 1798 rebellion. John died from wounds he received after the Battle of Ross.

In his later years, Doctor William Boxwell worked in Abbeyleix and became known as the 'Workhouse Doctor.' He was one of a few physicians that visited the poor in their own homes. His annual salary was 92 pounds 6 shillings and 2 pence. He attended upwards of 3,000 people each year. His district included Abbeyleix, Ballyroan, Clonenagh, Aghaboe, and Killermogh. The annual cost of the medicines' used during the year 1834 was listed as 30 pounds. Doctor Boxwell was held in high esteem by the people of Abbeyleix and at the surrounding areas at the time.

When Doctor William Boxwell died on the 8th of March 1845, his wife Sarah relocated to her daughters' residence at Richmond Park, Limerick a few years after her husband's death, and died there aged 83 years on the 9th of June 1883. The Boxwell family are buried in their own family plot in the old Church Graveyard in the Demesne in Abbeyleix. Unfortunately, the public do not have access to this site because of a decision that was made by the previous owners prior to the Collisions taken up residence there.

Anybody that has an interest in Genealogy will find the story of this Boxwell family from Sarshill in Wexford after 1798 a fascinating read. The history covers five centuries of this famous family. Doctor William Boxwell taught surgery to medical students while living in Woodville Abbeyleix, one of which was his half-brother, Francis.

One of his most notable medical students was a man named William, who later became known as Sir William Wilde. Wilde had become a noted Eye Surgeon. Born in Castlerea in Co Roscommon in March 1815, he died on April the 19th 1876. William Wilde went on to have six children, one of whom was the famous Irish poet, Oscar Wilde. Oscar Wilde died from Meningitis following an acute ear infection. He was born October 16th, 1854 and died on November the 30th 1900. His most famous poem was *The Ballad of Reading Gaol* written approximately three years before his death in the year 1900.
(Pictured: Thomas de Vesci, 7th Viscount)

Hung in Oldtown Abbeyleix

I was born and reared in Abbeyleix all my life, and as someone that has always been interested in history, especially local history, I must admit that I have never heard the story about the people hung in Abbeyleix until 2012. I am sure that I am not the only one from this area that finds themselves in the same position. Documenting history and stories about our past is so important, and we do it so that the generations who follow are informed and kept up to date about things that have happened in the past, both good and bad. The world needs to learn from the past so as not to repeat the same mistakes in the future.

The Three Priests
The Franciscan Friars were inspired by the 13th century St. Francis of Assisi. Born in 1182, St. Francis was a child of privilege. Being the son of a wealthy cloth merchant born in central Italy, Francis

felt that his life lacked meaning and abandoned his lifestyle to follow the word of God. He believed that he was asked by God to go and repair the Church and spread the word of God.

Before long, this itinerant beggar-preacher became widely known for his holiness, his empathy for the poor, and his radical self-giving to the Lord. Some were amused but many were inspired by his love of creation. Francis considered himself a small part of a remarkable universe inhabited by animals and elements that were all connected as 'brothers and sisters.' Many put aside their possessions and joined him to preach the Gospel. By the time Francis died in 1226, thousands of men had cast away their material possessions to become his brother friars, assuming the vows of poverty, chastity, and obedience. Many of the Franciscan brothers had other vocations such as doctors, lawyers, cobblers, tailors, or musicians.

Ireland had its own Franciscans priests, preaching the word of God. Three such priests were named John O' Molloy, Cornelius O' Doherty, and Geoffrey O' Farrell. They were proud Irishmen with a strong faith. The three Franciscan priests were recorded as having operated for eight years, preaching the word of God in remote areas of Wexford, Wicklow, Carlow, and Laois. They secretly celebrated Mass and ministered to the people in the Abbeyleix area, as well as other places throughout Leinster.

Persecution of the Irish People

Religious persecution in Ireland began under King Henry VIII, when local Parliament adopted acts establishing the King's ecclesiastical supremacy, abolishing the pope's jurisdiction, and suppressing religious houses. The act against the Pope came into operation on the 1st of November 1537. Its penalties were sufficiently terrible, but the licence of those enforcing it was more terrible still. They began burning down houses, destroying churches, killing priests that refused to erase their name from the canon of the mass, and tortured and killed preachers who did not repudiate the Pope's authority.

The three Priests travelled around the Leinster area mostly under the cover of darkness, preaching the word of God. The priests knew only too well what their fate would be if they were caught preaching the word of God. Catholicism was still against the law in this country during the reign of Queen Elizabeth I. Queen Elizabeth I's reign marked the turning point in the history of Ireland in all aspects of nationality language, laws, customs, and policy. It was the great wars of this reign that finally broke the power of the native chiefs and paved the way for English supremacy. The war was conducted by Carew, Gilbert, Pelham, and Mountjoy. Its object, according to the testimony of Lecky, was to exterminate the native race.

The slaughter of Irishmen was looked upon as quite literally the slaughter of wild beasts. Not only the men, but even the women and children who fell into the hands of the English, were deliberately and systematically butchered. Queen Elizabeth reigned from 1558 to 1603, during a period called the Elizabethan age. She was born in Greenwich near London in September 1533 and died in Surrey in 1603. During her time in power, England had asserted itself vigorously as a major European power in politics.

Reading on may be a little uncomfortable for some people.

Beginning of the End
According to tradition, Fate caught up with the Priests while they were travelling through what is now called, County Laois. The three priests were overtaken by a party of cavalry, bound hand and foot, brought back to a military garrison in Abbeyleix, not as it is known today but rather in Oldtown Abbeyleix. Their crime was that they were Catholic priests who had celebrated Mass for the local people among others. Reports at the time say that the priests were beaten with sticks, scourged with whips, before being offered rich rewards to abandon their beliefs, which all three rejected.

The three priests were then taken out of the garrison in Oldtown, where they were hung, drawn, and quartered by the English on the 15th of December 1588. Their remains were then burnt and buried in Oldtown. The martyrdom site is located 300 meters nearer to the Town of Abbeyleix on the Ballacolla road, from the memorial. This memorial is located on the green, as it is known locally, which is opposite the old post office at Oldtown Abbeyleix. It has taken

424 years for the story about the Priests to be told. These were three very brave men, that gave up their lives for believing in their faith.

Mass was celebrated in the Church of the most holy rosary in Abbeyleix before the memorial was unveiled by Fr Joseph Mc Mahon along with our local clergy. The memorial was erected by Mr John Moore, Ballinakill Road Abbeyleix in 2012. Information was provided by the Heritage House, Billy Quinn from main street Abbeyleix and others. Part of this history was recorded by The Rev John Cannon O' Hanlon, P.P. M.R.I.A. The first volume of his book was published in 1907, two years after the death of the author.

Abbeyleix Golf Club History - From Inception to Present Day

In 1895, Abbeyleix Golf Club was established by a small group of enthusiastic residents of the town and its surrounding areas. Little is known of the general membership in the early years, as minute books and other records of the club could not be located. From occasional newspaper clippings of the time, the 5th Viscount de Vesci was installed as a permanent club President, and the Secretary was a local Rector Rev'd A. E. Bor, who seemed to be the driving force in the club for the first twenty years or so. It is not known exactly where the first course was established.

Local legend states that golf was initially played in the area known as 'The Island' situated between the Portlaoise and Ballyroan roads. Stories tell of golf balls being dug up there on occasion. In 1905, the Abbeyleix Golf Club was affiliated to the Golfing Union of Ireland, under the captaincy of Mr. Hampton, Headmaster of The Preston School in Abbeyleix. Around this time, the club moved to a self-made course in the Ballymullen area where it continued for some time. Records indicate that Abbeyleix Golf Club was one of only two known golf clubs in Laois at this time, the other was located in Portarlington.

During this time, the Club had just two trophies to be played for each year - The Ballymullen Cup and The de Vesci Cup. The first recorded winner of the Ballymullen Cup was Miss J. Stoney in 1907. Both men and women were regarded as full members of the club, and both played in all competitions. In the 1920 edition of the Dunlop Book the Motorists guide, Abbeyleix Golf Club was described as a nine-hole course, green fees 2 shillings (about ten cents) per day, but no play was allowed on Sundays.

Abbeyleix Golf Club moved many times during the first 25 years of its existence for a variety of reasons. The first documented move occurred in 1921 when the record of a special meeting adopted a motion, "that owing to repeated wilful damage to the course in Ballymullen, the Links be closed and the Club would play competitions on Colonel Hugo Poe's course in Heywood," Ballinakill. Records also show that there were 24 members in the club and that on average, 14 of them played in the major competitions. A point of interest, during these times, both player and marker had to sign their cards after each hole was played.

Heywood Golf Course 1921

'Bogey For Heywood'. The word Bogey at that time was used to describe the Par for the course.

1st Hole	The Bridge	Bogey	4	205 yds.
2nd	Oak	Bogey	5	325 yds
3rd	Temple Hill	Bogey	3	77 yds
4th	Lough	Bogey	5	311 yds
5th	Curley	Bogey	4	247 yds
6th	Cross Road	Bogey	5	278 yds
7th	Castle	Bogey	4	232 yds
8th	The Basin	Bogey	3	82 yds
9th	Tree & Mounds	Bogey	4	234 yds

During the twenties, committee meetings minutes show that the cost of maintaining the Heywood course was about £15 a year. Greens were cut once a week during the summer months and only once a month during the winter. Fairways were rolled about once a month and interestingly they did not need to be cut as the course was grazed by cattle for most of the year.

In 1923, it was decided, that in major competitions where ladies were playing on the same tees as men, an extra quarter should be added to the ladies' handicaps. As a result, various ladies won the major competitions for the next couple of years. After two years an A.G.M. decided to add two shots to all handicaps. In 1925, the first Captain's Prize was introduced by Captain of the year Colonel Marsden. The committee chose the prize, which was nine golf balls. During the 1920s, membership grew slowly, reaching 40 in 1927. However, the annoyance of having to travel to Heywood and the cost of maintaining the course there led to another move. For the first time the Club moved to Rathmoyle. Mr Robert Wilde of Rathmoyle House, offered the lawn in front of his house as a course for a fee of no more than ten guineas. The course was officially opened on the 11th of May 1927. 1929 saw the employment of a professional for a few weeks to assist members to improve their game. Later that year, the first recorded inter-club competition was held against Portarlington Golf Club. No record exists of the result.

The Ladies of the club formed their own section in 1930 and elected their own secretary who was granted an automatic seat on the Club Committee. Later that year, the Ladies were affiliated to the I.L.G.U. for a fee of one guinea. The year 1930 also witnessed what must have been one of the epic contests in the Golf Club's history. The captain made his captains prize a match-play competition. The prize was won by W.T. White who defeated his opponent P. Cahill on the ninth tie hole, the 27th in all. Once again, the cost of maintenance, resulted in a move back to Ballymullen which took place in October 1932.

Abbeyleix Golf Club settled back in Ballymullen by the middle of the 1930s. Having leased some extra acres, a full nine-hole course was established and a professional from Rathdowney was employed to lay out the new course. An inter club match with Johnstown Golf club was arranged to formalize the opening of the new course. The general economic depression of the thirties created difficulties for the club and membership declined slowly with non-payment of subscriptions adding to the problems. By the end of 1933, the financial situation forced the committee to end the lease for the course and close the club, at least on a temporary basis. A few of the more enthusiastic committee members negotiated with Robert

Wilde and succeeded in having a winter course only available from November 1934 to May 1935 initially.

The 1937 Annual General Meeting decided that the Officers and committee were elected unchanged. However, by May of that year the membership reluctantly decided to close the club and course indefinitely. The committee elected three trustees to take charge of all club property and finance. The trustees arranged for the club's trophies and minute books to be lodged in a local bank. The club's machinery was put in the care of a local farmer. All this was done with an eye on a better future and a re-opening of the club when conditions improved. With the onset of World War II, it would be over ten years before their dreams would come true.

A New Beginning

In 1948, as life began to return to normal, the pre-war members began to look at the possibility of reopening the Golf club. A public meeting was called which was attended by 28 prospective members, and the decision was taken to re-establish the old course at Rathmoyle. Both Ladies and Men's sections were established with officers and committees elected. Very little change was made to the old nine-hole course and an aluminium clubhouse was erected on the site of the present-day building. All work was voluntary, and proceeded so well that the first competition, a nine-hole mixed, was held on Sunday the 31st of October 1948.

To raise much needed funds, a series of functions were arranged, particularly by the Ladies' section. The most successful of these was an annual carnival week in the town during which marquee dancing was held in the town park with the top dance and show bands of the time. It provided great entertainment and was hugely popular. By June 1949, the clubhouse obtained its liquor license and a bar was installed. The golf club was affiliated to the Golfing Union of Ireland in October, but were informed by the Union, that Ladies could only be associated members. By way of compensation to the Ladies, the committee provided many cups and prizes to the Ladies' section and facilities to play their competitions. The Ladies' section affiliated to the I.L.G.U. at the same time. By

1951, membership had increased to over 40 and the clubhouse became a social centre for the town.

In October 1951, the officers and committee arranged for a group of well-known Irish International amateur golfers, including Joe Carr, who later became Captain of the R&A at St. Andrews, to play an exhibition match in Abbeyleix. Golfers from all over Laois came to watch but unfortunately the persistent and torrential rain limited the enjoyment of players and spectators alike. Later that evening, lively discussions in the clubhouse allayed an otherwise unpleasant golfing experience. Carr still managed a round of 73 in the torrid conditions.

About the same time, Abbeyleix Golf Club joined forces with the clubs in Carlow and Mountrath to initiate the South Leinster inter-club competition. With team members of 18 handicap and over, Abbeyleix played in the competition almost every year since. The competitive nature of the membership at this time is evident from minutes of a committee where a resolution was passed, "seriously urging members to be more careful in their choice of language on the course."

In 1959, a local rule was introduced which stated, "that players could shelter during any competition," which was not in line with GUI ruling, and had to be withdrawn within a year or so. In 1964, the Ladies section invited the most renowned and respected Lady Golfer, Philomena Garvey, to spend a day at the club, playing and giving lessons on the art of good play. Philomena was Ireland's first Lady Professional Golfer and Abbeyleix was one of the first Golf Clubs she visited as a professional player. Many Ladies and indeed men learned a great deal from the experience and an entertaining evening followed.

A New Era

1970 saw the introduction of the Golfer of the year award for the first time. The following year in a spirit of generosity and friendship, when the Heath Golf Club suffered major problems with their greens, they were invited to play their major competitions in Abbeyleix. At this time, with the development of the Abbeyleix Festival the club introduced the May-time Open week to be run in conjunction with the event. Both the

Festival and Open week rapidly became enormously successful as a major sporting and social event in the Midlands.

While several minor changes to the course occurred over the years, the major improvement came in 1976. The increase in usage called for a green watering system to be installed to maintain the high standard of the course. A Well, over 100ft deep, was sunk adjacent to the clubhouse and with a great deal of voluntary help from the membership, pipes were laid to all greens, with four sprinklers around each green. An electronic switching device ensured that the greens were automatically watered in sequence and for the time required for each green. An ever-increasing number of young golfers began to play. A Juvenile and Junior section was established in the club. In time, regular lessons were set up and a fixtures list of local competitions and inter-club matches were introduced. Many club members today owe the development of their golfing ability to those happy days and the mentors of the Juvenile and Junior sections.

Towards the end of the 1970's, the increased membership and the ever- increasing number of visiting players led to the building of new locker rooms and toilets at the end of the old clubhouse. This was followed by the demolition of the old aluminium structure and the building of several modifications at various times, forming the basis of the facilities that exist today. To raise revenue and assist the club's financial position, several new ventures were undertaken. The club began to open its doors to golfing societies, particularly from Dublin. A day's golfing for a society followed by a meal and evening in the bar proved to be very profitable. The introduction of the Celebrity Classics benefited the finances too. For one day a year, the club played host to many of the prominent members of the entertainment world and their friends. The course was filled with happy celebrities and members playing golf during the day and the clubhouse rang out with song and laughter long into the night. In recognition of the major working contribution made by the Lady members of the club, the committee decided to remove from the constitution of the club the rule restricting Ladies to associate membership and gave them the option of becoming full members if they so wished. Abbeyleix was one of the first clubs in the country to begin the process of eliminating such discrimination.

The new clubhouse was officially opened by officers from the Men's and Ladies Golfing Unions of Ireland in 1980 and the next decade saw the standard of golf played in Abbeyleix reach new heights. Among the Lady members, one became an Irish International player winning several caps, another winning the Midland Championship for Ladies, and many were involved in winning mixed teams which represented the club in inter-club competition. Notably, the Cullen Cup against a very fancied Dublin opposition. The men's section also had its successes. Among them were the National All-Ireland singles champion and the National Four-ball champions. Abbeyleix members were frequently selected for Laois in inter county matches with much success.

Continuous attention was applied to improving the course both from a golfing and an appearance point of view. Planting of spinneys and trees achieved both purposes, to such an extent that Abbeyleix was asked by the G.U.I. on many occasions to host the semi-finals and finals of inter-club competition. A rare occurrence for a club with a nine-hole course. Throughout these years, the members of Abbeyleix became well known in clubs all over Leinster as many travelled regularly to Open Days and such like, Tramore Open week being a particular attraction for many years. In response, members of these clubs regularly attended Open weeks in Abbeyleix, and in time, to accommodate the increased numbers attending, the 'Open Week' became a ten-day event.

In the early 1990s, the club joined with the other Laois clubs in instituting a Golfing Day for the Captains and past Captains, Ladies and Men. These social days were held annually on the June Bank Holiday and hosted in clubs all around South Leinster. They consisted of an 18-hole competition, an evening meal, and a musical evening. In time, many other clubs joined the group, and the event gave the legends of the club game a unique opportunity to exchange reminiscences and provide happy memories for one and all.

In January 1992, the respect with which Abbeyleix Golf club was held by all surrounding clubs became very evident when an act of vandalism resulted in all the greens being seriously damaged to such an extent that all had to be totally replaced. Help was immediately offered by almost all the surrounding clubs from Portarlington to Kilkenny, with the offer of machinery, manpower, greenkeepers, etc. With their invaluable help and a huge voluntary effort by Abbeyleix members, the greens were as good as new within nine months.

During the first half of this decade, membership began to increase considerably, with many young new members joining the ranks. To assist beginners, a Monday evening Mixed Foursome was established, where each experienced member formed a team with a beginner for nine holes. They explained the rules and regulations on the way round, the 'etiquette' of golf, and helped them improve their golf in any way possible. The whole concept was very popular, and many long-term friendships became established as a result.

Centenary Year 1995
The year 1995 brought Abbeyleix Golf club to its centenary year. The event was acknowledged in many and various ways. By coincidence the town of Abbeyleix gained the status of Laois Heritage Town the same year, so both town and club had reason to celebrate. Among other golf clubs which celebrated their centenary the same year were Massereene Golf Club in

Northern Ireland, and Cosby Golf Club from Leicestershire in England. Both were contacted and home and away days of celebration were arranged with both. Many celebrities from the world of entertainment attended and long evenings of entertainment ensued. The Abbeyleix members, who paid return visits to both clubs, were welcomed, and royally entertained in similar manner.

Many new members joined because of the centenary celebrations. This in turn, led to the consideration of increasing the size of the course from its historical nine holes to a possible 18 hole. Work began in 1998 to extend the course to 18 holes. Various meetings were arranged to establish what land was available and several international course designers were invited to submit plans for consideration. These designers visited Abbeyleix and were taken on numerous tours of the property. When the designs had been studied at length, an Emergency General Meeting decided on those submitted by Mr Mel Flanagan, which is the course in existence today.

The next couple of years saw the new course developing, with water features and spinneys appearing and new fairways and greens being laid out. For many months, those walking the course spent more time admiring the new developments than actually playing golf! It was with great excitement that the opening of the course in 2000 was celebrated. A fitting start to herald the incoming new millennium. With the combined club membership, the ladies and men climbed to the 500 mark, a far cry from the handful of determined folk who fought their own fights and won their own battles time after time, to give us the clubhouse and course that exists today. Now as the club moves through the new millennium, its members can take great pride in it and be very grateful to all those stalwarts who over the years, with their enthusiasm and energy, built the amenity which is enjoyed by one and all today.

The New Course
The key to Mel Flanagan's success was working his design around the boundaries of the course rather than being confined by attempting to keep the existing course intact as favoured by

many members. His first hole started from a new tee situated near the clubhouse to the existing fourth, which was the saucer green at the time. That brave decision unlocked the secret to the remainder of the route map. Holes 2 to 8 and 12 inclusive were on new land areas while1, 9, 16, 17, 11 and 15 occupied lands from new and existing areas. The course was designed so that when you stood on the course's vantage points, you could view the beautiful surrounding scenery as well. It is now a challenge to the existing members to avail of the great potential that this fine 18 Hole golf course has to offer towards increasing our membership and visitor numbers.

Official Opening of New Course

The official opening of the new course, by Mr Patrick Murphy, President of the G.U.I. took place on Sunday, 17th September 2000. Dermot Gilleece's article in the Sports Page of the Irish Times one year later (5th June 2001) described our new course as magnificent and having a new layout that is a suitable test for real golfers. Looking back over my time as a member of Abbeyleix Golf Club, a lot of hard-working members stand out and deserve to be thanked and praised for their hard work and dedication to the club. Of course, there are far too many to mention!

I'm thinking back to when I first joined as a member of the golf club, and I remember people like Hughie Cole who worked tirelessly on the course often using his own machinery when the club wasn't able to buy their own. The green keeper that had to work single-handedly at the time, trying to keep the golf course in playing condition at all times, as well as keeping the clubhouse painted and everything else in between. He was none other than Joey Rogers from Rathmoyle. Joey deserved great credit and received the same from all the members of the club at the time for all his efforts. Joey was eventually joined by his lifelong friend Tom Lodge who helped him to keep the golf course in ship shape condition, especially when Joeys health began to fail.

Another man that deserves special recognition for being a playing member in the Golf club for the last 71 years and continues to play competitively, he is a very popular member and much loved by all of the present and past members of the club, he is none other than the very well-known A. J. Cole from upper main street in Abbeyleix. A. J. quoted and documented a few versus from Longfellow's poem 'Footprints on the Sands of Time' as a thank you to the members that worked so hard to bring about this change, going from a nine-hole golf course to that of an 18 hole one.

(And I quote)

Lives of great men all remind us
We can make our lives sublime,
And departing leave behind us
Footprints on the sands of time".

"Not enjoyment and not sorrow,
Is our destined end or way|
But to act, that each tomorrow
Find us farther than today".

"Let us then be up and doing
With a heart for any fate,
Still achieving, still pursuing,
Learn to labour and to wait.

A Stalwart of the Club

Probably the best in my opinion and the most successful golfer Abbeyleix Golf club has ever produced, throughout its long history over 127 years is perhaps Peter Rogers. I have had the good fortune to research this gentleman's achievements since he joined the golf club in 1958. Peter has been a dedicated and much-admired member of the golf club since he first joined. He has held both of the

top positions in the club. He was captain in the year 2000 when the club progressed from a nine-hole course to18. In 2014, he became President. In addition, Peter held the position of golf club secretary during the 1970s.

When Peter joined the club, he played golf on that first Christmas day in 1958, and he has continued to play golf on each and every Christmas day since. He is looking forward to playing golf for this Christmas day 2022 which will be his 65th outing without fail! It all started when he left Christmas day Mass along with Mick Mc Grath from Rathmoyle in 1958. Mick asked Peter to go to the golf course and play a few holes of golf before dinner time, and so this record began which probably will never be broken by anyone. On an unforgettable Christmas day 2010, not only Abbeyleix golf course but the whole country was covered in a blanket of snow, but this did not stop Peter continuing with his tradition. He went to the golf course and managed to play a couple of holes, granted he lost a few golf balls. This feat was captured by our very well-known photographer James G Carroll, producing a beautiful photo with Peters footprints in the snow on that Christmas day.

Peter along with some of his other friends played golf with pot sticks in the Convent field in their earlier years. They improvised by using bean cans buried in the ground, placing a rag on top of a stick, and using them as a flagpole in a nine-hole golf course that they had created in the field. In 1958, Peter decided to join the Golf club in Abbeyleix. He was earning 10 shillings a week at the time working as a young lad in Bramley's garage in the town. Membership subscription was £3 at the time. He saved up the membership fee, joined the club but unfortunately still had no golf clubs with which to play.

Around this time, Pat Cruite, a saddler that had a shop on the Ballinakill road in the town was retiring from his work and moving to Dublin. Peter went to him and asked if he was selling his golf clubs. Pat Cruite wanted 30 shillings for them. Peter agreed to purchase them but needed to save up. He eventually bought the golf clubs which consisted of 5 irons, from a 3 iron down, with hickory shafts and a putter. There were no woods in the set, so by Christmas of 1958 he was ready to play golf. Peter in his first full year as a member in 1959 won the Ballymullen cup. He also won the Captains Prize in the same year. He won the de Vesci cup a total of six times. The first one in 1960 alongside winning the Vice Captains prize in the same year. Incidentally the last de Vesci cup Peter won in 2017 was presented by the 7th Viscount de Vesci. This was an important occasion because it was the first time this cup was presented by the current Viscount. He also won the captains prize in 1973, playing off a handicap of three.

Matchplay singles competition he won on four occasions. In 1971, he successfully defended the first one he won in 1970. The other two occasions were in 1976 and 1986. Peter was also a member of Thurles Golf Club in his earlier years. He represented both Abbeyleix and Thurles in the Senior cup and the Barton Shield competitions in his time. Peter became a member of the Thurles Golf Club as his job took him down that direction and he was required to stay overnight at least one night a week. Peter played off a low handicap of only 2 when he represented his club and beat some well-known fancied golfers in his time. Some of which he beat on more than one occasion! Not too many golfers can say that they held the course record in four different golf courses during their lifetime, that of Abbeyleix, Castlecomer, the Heath, and Rathdowney.

When he scored a Hole-in-One on the first hole in an Open competition in Castlecomer in May 1968, he went on to break the course record by recording a score of 66! The course at the time measured 4,744- yards, Peter was playing off a handicap of 5 at the time. In September of that year, Peter broke the course record in Abbeyleix on no less than five separate occasions in the One Year, recording scores of 69, 68, 68, and 69. He had already reduced the course record to 71 earlier in the year. Peter has in his possession a golf ball named *Raxis* that was given to him by Tom Kirwan, a landowner from Ballymullen where the Abbeyleix Golf Club members played their golf prior to 1906. A golf ball named *Dunlop 65* is also in his possession so named, because the ball originally commemorated Sir Henry Cotton's second round of 65 in the 1934 Open Championship, when he went on to win the Claret Jug at Royal St George, Sandwich with a four-round total of 283.

Peter Rogers was the youngest member ever in the club to win a Senior men's Captains prize, and the oldest at 76 to win a major singles competition. He has won numerous competitions in between, far too many to mention. I don't know of any other golfer in the club that has a better record than that, and there are some very good golfers in the club.

Another Impressive Feat

An impressive golfing feat was carried out by another valued member of Abbeyleix Golf Club on the 25th of June 1982. Eugene Fennelly playing off 3 handicap on his home course played 200 holes of golf in aid of the Senior citizens of the Town. Eugene began his Golf Marathon at 4.50 am covering 45 miles. He was accompanied by various caddies throughout the day finally finishing at 10.24 pm. This was certainly a remarkable achievement. Eugene's average score after completing 200 holes of golf was 78.8 per round. The average time for 9 holes was 1 hour 32 minutes, and the fastest nine holes was completed in 31 minutes. Eugene also broke the course record on the old Abbeyleix course when he finished with a score of 65 Gross on the 21st of August 1983.

The 1920 Minute Book

Much of the detail of this article has been sourced in the 1920 Club Minute Book. This minute book deserves its place in the

Abbeyleix Heritage House Museum, it has been so meticulously kept that it has been possible for us to tell the history of this fantastic golf club. These great men and women officers and members of the past that were responsible for all of our members, and indeed visitors alike, enjoying this fabulous amenity today. This book contributed to the compilation of the history of Abbeyleix Golf club from the beginning in 1895 right up to 2022. Andrea Rogers a former Lady Captain & President and incidentally the wife of the aforementioned Peter Rogers cannot be thanked enough because she found this minute book along with others in a bin destined for the dump. What an absolute disaster that would have been!

Jack Delaney

Known as Jack Delaney, this Abbeyleix man's name is not officially Delaney but rather Jack Hill. The people of Abbeyleix would be much more aware of his relatives, that were Peter Rogers and Maisie Delaney. Employed as a nurse and as an assistant Matron later in her career in the Abbeyleix fever hospital, Maisie lived in a lovely little house down Tullyroe lane. When you walk or drive down Tullyroe, or otherwise known as Moran's Lane, just as you reach the old railway bridge, you'll find a road that sweeps down to the left. It takes you down to the back of the tennis court, and if you continue straight, you'll find that you pass the Sexton's house on your right-hand side and then end up at a junction. If you then go left, you're back into town, where-as if you go right, you are heading down to Sweet-view or on to Ballacolla. Maisie lived in this beautiful cottage situated right at the railway bridge along with her mother Mary and her aunt Winifred Delaney. This story as told by Maisie in her 85th year in 2019 is one that is well worth holding on to, so I've decided to document it, because it's a story about an Abbeyleix family, and hopefully people might enjoy reading it, as much as I have writing it.

Maisie's Father

It is a common tradition that when a man and a woman get married, the woman usually takes the man's name. On this occasion, the opposite was the case. When Maisie's mother Mary and her father Jack Hill met in the church to get married her father decide to take his wife's surname,

Delaney. It may have had something to do with the fact that Jack was a Protestant and Mary was a Roman Catholic, and so he became known from then on as John 'Jack' Delaney. And so, that's how he started his married life. Jack and Mary lived in number 16 Knocknamoe before moving to number 22 Tullyroe. Jack and Mary had one daughter who they named Maisie. The family loved living in Tullyroe. Maisie enjoyed going to school, playing with her friends, and quite often, to pass the time she would stand at the Railway bridge along with her aunt Winifred watching the trains enter and leave the station. There was an opening beside the bridge where Maisie would climb down occasionally with Winifred and play in the field close to the rail line, while her aunt would pick sticks, that had fallen on the railway tracks from off the trees that were growing in the ditch alongside the lane close by. They had great fun and marvellous memories from doing so.

Maisie's Nightmare

On the 24th of May 1949 at 7pm, their lives changed forever. While returning from town, Maisie saw Winifred climb down the bank beside the bridge as she had often done before and began to pick the sticks along the railway track in the same area as she had always done before. Maisie and her mother were in the house when they heard the screeching of brakes from the train.

"Oh My God," Maisie's mother screamed out, "something terrible has happened."

They both raced out of the house and across to the railway bridge. Her mother screamed out when she saw that her sister Winifred had been hit by the train and lay lifeless on the ground close to the railway line. Maisie's memory became faded at that point, and she could only remember being comforted by neighbours and friends some hours later. They struggled to come to terms with this awful tragedy for years after, the best they could do was to try and learn how to live with it. An inquest was held at a later time in the hospital in Abbeyleix. The jury was made up of some local men including Jn Thornton (foreman), Ed Purcell, Hugh O' Connor, W Shiel, T Cruite, T Coady, J Reilly, and Dr Duane coroner for Laois. It was explained to the jury that Winifred was described as a deaf mute, and it was most likely she did not see or hear the train coming. After the investigation, the train driver was exonerated from any blame. It was said to have just been an awful accident, and nobody was to blame. The funeral was one of the largest ever seen in Abbeyleix for a number of years. This story appeared on the front page of the Nationalist and Leinster Times on Saturday the 28th of May 1949, the same day as my own baby brother Michael died from meningitis.

The Silver Spoon
As Maisie wipes away the tears, she recalls the story about the silver spoon.
"Her father," she said, "Jack Delaney, or Jack Hill, Peter Rogers granduncle, when he was growing up, like lots of other young lads of his age, was unable to find a job, just because they were scarce."

This was now 1914, Jack came home one day and told his wife that he had just signed up to fight in the war. The First World War started in August of 1914 and there was a big recruitment drive going on, promising a great career in the army, with money, free uniforms, food, a new life, etc. So, like lots of other men, Jack signed his name on the dotted line. Jack packed his bags, and just before he left, his wife who didn't want him to go in the first place, gave him a new silver spoon, one that she would have kept in the parlour for when special visitors would call. One that the children of the house would never get an opportunity to use. So many of us can remember this practice in our own homes growing up, our own mothers keeping the parlour clean and tidy in case someone important came calling. His wife asked him to mind the spoon and bring it back home with him after the war. And so he made a promise to his wife to do so.

Fighting the war In Europe

At the beginning of the war, Jack was one of 30,000 men that signed up to fight in the First World War in 1914. Irish soldiers that fought in the war were engaged on many fronts from Belgium and France to the Greek port of Salonika and from Gallipoli to Palestine. They suffered heavy losses in this war. The 16th Irish divisions participated in the huge British offensive at the Somme from July to December 1916. Most of the soldiers that fought in those wars, spent a lot of their time in the trenches, in the muck, rain, heat, and frost. The soldiers eating their food had to eat for the most part while they were in the trenches, primarily using their hands and fingers. Jack while in the trenches ate his food using the spoon that his wife had given him. Some 35,000 Irish soldiers perished in this war. For a small country, Ireland constituted a substantial sacrifice and a significant contribution to the Allied cause.

Finally, when 1918 came around, the end of the war was in sight. Jack thought of seeing home again. On the 11th of November 1918 the war ended, and Jack made it back to Abbeyleix just before Christmas time. Having lost a lot of weight, being tired and worn out, Jack eventually made it to the front door. He was greeted by his wife who was overjoyed to see her husband arrive back home in one piece, because all she had heard on the radio over the previous four years was about all the soldiers that were losing their lives over there. When Jack had finished hugging his wife Mary, he put his hand in his pocket and pulled out the silver spoon that his wife had given him before going off to fight in the war.

"I told you that I would bring you back the spoon," he said. Mary Delaney told the story about the silver spoon to her daughter Maisie and asked her to cherish this spoon and never let anything happen to it. Maisie kept the spoon safe all her life and decided to leave it to one of her relations, someone she really trusts and knows that the spoon will be looked after.

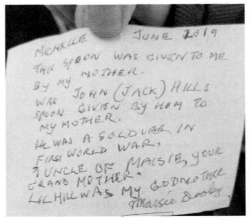

Now that Maisie is in her 86th year she wanted her story to be told and sent for Michelle, a daughter of Andrea and Peter Rogers. Maisie explained her story and gave Michelle a written explanation about the silver spoon. She placed the written note along with the spoon in a bag and just said "please mind it."

I believe this has been a beautiful, sad, and tragic story, about Maisie's life and one that I was honoured to have been told about. I knew Maisie Delaney while growing up in Abbeyleix, a nice woman. She married later in life, moved away from Abbeyleix along with her husband Tom Dooley and lived her life in Durrow, Co Laois. Maisie suffered a bad accident in 2012. She was knocked down while crossing the road and continues to suffer as a result of that accident even to this day. Unfortunately, Maisie's husband Tom died early in the Spring of 2021 at 86 years of age. And sadly, Maisie died on the 20th of November 2021.

Pictured: Peter Rogers

James Delaney

A Story of True Heroism

James Delaney was an Abbeyleix man awarded the Distinguished Conduct Medal (DCM) with bar due to his heroic efforts during the First World War. The DCM was an extremely high-level award for bravery. Bars were awarded to the DCM in recognition of the performance of further acts of gallantry meriting the award. A story of courage and bravery in the First World War was recalled at the funeral of Mr James Delaney. His unexpected death caused widespread shock in his community when he died at his Ballymena home in Antrim, December 1960. He was 66 years old.

Mr James Delaney was the son of Mr and Mrs Thomas Delaney of Ballymaddock, Abbeyleix. James was one of thirteen children, some of which were born in Temperance Street and others in Ballymaddock, in a little three-bedroom house situated on the right-hand side of the road just as you pass Thornberry Estate and move into Ballymaddock. James's father, Thomas, was a soldier in the British Army as was one of his other sons. James decided to follow suit and signed up. James was given an official Army Registration number 10492 only later to be dismissed and sent home because he gave a false date of birth. To become a British soldier, he needed to be 18 years of age. James' mother managed to get him back home to Abbeyleix which made her very happy.

When World War I began in 1914, the British Army began a huge recruitment campaign in Ireland. About 140,000 Irish signed up to fight alongside the British. They signed up as soldiers of the Royal Irish Regiment. These soldiers, which included about 4,500 women, set off and played their part in the fight against the German Army that moved into France in August 1914 effectively starting what became known as the Great War. James had seen this as a great opportunity to try and sign up again, and so off he went. On this occasion he was accepted into the British Army and given the Registration number 10494. James was regarded as quite a good soldier and it didn't take long before he was promoted to a Lance Corporal.

He became a sergeant shortly after that, which was the rank he had achieved when he landed in France to fight in the war.

When Sergeant James Delaney served with the Royal Irish Regiment in WW1, he engaged in an encounter with the Prussian Guards, a crack German Regiment. His Commanding Officer was killed, and although severely wounded himself, Sgt Delaney took command and led his men to take the towns of Ginchy and Guillemont. His own father and brother were under his command in this adventure. The Battle of Ginchy took place on the 9th of September 1916 during the Battle of the Somme, when the 16th Irish Division captured the German held village. Several German counter attacks were defeated. The loss of Ginchy deprived the Germans of observation posts from which they could observe the battlefield. Ginchy is a commune in the Somme in Hauts-de-France. It is situated in Northern France and had a very small population living there at the time.

The Allied victory at the Somme, despite its horrific costs, inflicted serious damage on German positions in France, spurring the Germans to strategically retreat to the Hindenburg Line in March 1917 rather than continue battling over the same land that spring. The exact numbers of losses by the end of the Battle of the Somme have been disputed. The Germans reputed to have lost 450,000 soldiers compared to 420,000 for the British. The surviving British soldiers gained valuable experience, which would help them later to achieve ultimate victory on the Western Front.

The Villages of Ginchy and Guillemont in the Somme region of France joined to commemorate the courageous efforts and grievous losses suffered by the 16th Irish Division to liberate both villages from German occupation in September 1916. James Delaney was offered a commission as a result of his actions during this war but refused it, determined that he wanted to stay with his men. James Delaney later had his arm amputated due to the injuries he received from the gun shots that were inflicted at the Battle of Ginchy.

End of the War
Jack Delaney, no relation of James, was from Tullyroe, Abbeyleix who also signed up as a soldier at the beginning of

World War I, and incidentally joined the same regiment as James. His father William and brothers Chris and Patrick Delaney, remained at home in Ballymaddock, Abbeyleix. They all signed up and became members of the British Army and the Royal Irish Regiment in particular. They set off to fight against the German Army who had taken over several towns and villages in France in 1914. The war eventually ended on the 11th of November 1918. Jack made it home just before Christmas 1918.

When James Delaney returned home to his mother in late 1916 after the Battle of Ginchy, he had a long way to go, trying to recuperate from the life changing injuries he received during the war. James spent several months recuperating from his injuries. He married a local lady named Mollie Cummins from Temperance in 1917. The war ended by November 1918 and work became difficult to find. James and Mollie had one daughter named Mary which made their situation difficult trying to survive. Work became even more scarce the following year when the War of Independence broke out and subsequently the Civil War. The fact that James only had one arm certainly didn't help his case. James headed to Dublin to find work. There he encountered a man who offered him work in a linen factory doing office work. The only problem was that the work was in Ballymena in Antrim. In 1927, James made his way to the North of Ireland to Antrim.

James Heads North
James, Mollie, and their daughter got the train to Antrim. They eventually arrived in Ballymena. He did not know a single soul there, so he decided to search for a Priest to ask where he could find lodgings. The Priest asked him various questions, James informed him that he had a job to go to.

When he told the Priest where the job was, the Priest said, "Son, go back home. That's a terrible place. No Catholics are employed there, you wouldn't survive."

James replied, "I have a wife and child to support, I need a job."

James went to where his employment was and started work. The other employees began bullying and intimidating him because he was a Catholic. Eventually the other employees began to respect him because they learned that he fought for the British in the war and lost his arm in the process. James was promoted in the job sometime later and settled down and began to enjoy where he was living. James and Mollie had a son in 1924 whom they named Thomas. James always wore a Poppy on the 11th of November and marched proudly to the war memorial in Ballymena every year, even though some of the Priests preached from the pulpit that Catholics shouldn't! James never spoke about his time in the war.

When World War II broke out in September 1939, their son Thomas joined the RAF at a young age. He went to war just as his father did in the First World War. Thomas was killed in action in the Battle for Britain at only 21 years of age. His son's death was something that James never got over for the rest of his life. James continued to march to the war memorial in Ballymena on the 11th of November each year remembering all his fallen comrades including his own son Thomas. James died in 1960. After a short illness, James's wife Mollie died in 1968.

Mr Chris Delaney

James' brother, Chris Delaney, was a well-known man in the Abbeyleix community. He lived with his wife Eileen and their eight children in a house which had previously been used as a school in the early 1900s. The house was widely known as Bluegate, Killamuck, Abbeyleix. Chris worked as a butler in the Abbeyleix House for the De Vesci Family for most of his working life. His children were all educated in Abbeyleix, before they moved on to live in various parts of the country and indeed New York and London also.

Thom

One of Chris's sons was called Thomas, but spelt his name as 'Thom.' Thom joined the Army after leaving school and served in the Congo and Cyprus. When he left the army, he took up a job as a bus conductor in Dublin. While working there he attended night classes and studied drama at the Brendan Smith Academy. He later moved to London and enrolled in a drama school for two years full-time. He worked in a variety of jobs to support himself during this time.

His first break as a professional actor came in children's theatre and from there, he moved into repertory theatre working all over England with different companies. In London, he appeared in the West End and played frequently on television in series such as '*Crossroads*' and '*Thriller.*' It was while working in London that his fellow-actor, Nicholas Amer, suggested that he should put together a one-man show based on Irish material. And so '*The Importance of Being Irish*' was born.

Thom Delaney set about gathering material for the show and soon had enough for a performance that would last over 30 hours. After ruthless pruning, the show was condensed to just over two hours and had its first public performance in 1979 at St. Andrew's in Scotland under Nicholas Amer's direction. The show, which was then called 'A Touch of Blarney', went down well with the Scottish audiences and one reviewer praised Delaney's performance for its combination of "different charm, considerable acting ability and stylish panache."

Putting the show together and memorising the material was an achievement in itself but finding a London theatre that would present it took what Thom describes as "a great deal of blood sweat and toil." The effort was well worth it.

Emphasis on Comedy

It was 'standing room only' as Thom Delaney took to the stage before an audience of 300, including some of the staff of the Irish Embassy. The emphasis was on comedy in the first half of the show and the extract from Frank O' Connor's story '*First Confession*' got the evening off to an excellent start with Delaney's sharp characterisations and subtle comedy in the narration. From there on, the audience warmed to his individual style of humour and his versatility in interpreting a wide range of material. Drawing on poetry of Yeats, Kavanagh, Myles na Gopaleen, Jennifer Johnston, and the plays of Shaw and Synge he presented a wide spectrum of Irish life. His choice of material coupled with his own contagious brand of humour and his obvious enjoyment of songs like '*Never Wed an Old Man*' had the audience firmly on his side by the end of the first hour.

The second half of the show opened with a comic routine that showed Delaney's skill as a stand-up comedian. Throughout the show he linked the various items with his own stories and anecdotes from his days as a bus conductor in Dublin and almost brought the house down with his telling of the tall yarn about the horse that played cricket. A change of mood came with his introduction of a selection of poems by Northern poets that tried to reflect the tragedy of the violence and killing there. Through the poems of Montague, Simmons and Fiacc and the children's poems on the war, Thom highlighted the darker, tragic side of Irish Life. The selection of material was interesting and original even if the tragic note shattered the comic mood rather too abruptly. By the end of the evening the audience had seen a highly individual and entertaining look at Ireland and the Irish-comic, ironic, tragic, sometimes sentimental, always interesting.

As a feat of memory and acting ability alone, Thom Delaney's achievement in this one-man show was impressive but it was his own obvious enjoyment of his material that gave the performance its vitality and won the enthusiastic applause of the audience at the end. He hoped to find a London Theatre where the show could have a longer uninterrupted run and after his successful short season at the Round House that looked very likely. His ambition was to bring the show to the Dublin Theatre Festival in October 1978 because he felt that an Irish audience would be the real test - "Perhaps they would crucify me", he said. Beyond that, there was the possibility of an American tour, and he was keeping his fingers crossed on that account. He was quietly optimistic and modest about his success, but one certainty was that the show would surface again, whether in London, Dublin, or New York.

'*The Importance of Being Irish*' tried to present a comprehensive view of Ireland as seen through the eyes of our most famous writers. The reaction of London audiences and critics was enthusiastic. The drama critic of London's weekly magazine '*Time Out*' wrote that Delaney's way with an audience was disarming and concluded his review by saying -

"Nobody with the smallest capacity for joy should miss this marvellous feat of memory, timing and taste."

Thom is Interviewed in March 1980

In a newspaper interview in March 1980, Thom spoke candidly about his career and where he wanted to take his one-man show. The headline in the newspaper article read – 'Thom has the London audiences laughing.'

He was now in his second week of his show in the Young Vic Studio. Thom was packing them in. It was almost three years since he first went on stage with his solo performance, and since then had great successes with it in Scotland, London, South Africa, and London again. But he complained that Ireland is the one country he had not been able to do the show in.

"I've approached the Abbey and the Peacock and the Project and no one is interested. Neither is Brendan Smith. They seem to think the show is too Irish," Thom said.

Thom 33 years of age in 1980 claimed that Abbeyleix was famous for nothing but himself! His show included yarns from his time in the Army when he served in the Congo and Cyprus and from the two and a half years he spent as a bus conductor in Dublin, and as well as that he recited poetry and extract from Shaw, Wilde, Synge, Yeats, Patrick Kavanagh, and Brendan Behan. Not only did he act and write, but he also sang too.

In 1987, Chris spent eight weeks in St Mary's hospital in the Phoenix Park Dublin where he passed away at the age of 75 years. He was survived by his wife Eileen Delaney, his sons Chris in Limerick, Laurence in Malahide, Dublin, Pat in Palmerstown, Dublin, Gerard in London, and Thomas in New York. His daughters Mrs Elizabeth Shiels resided at Palmerstown, and Mrs Anne Costello lived in Abbeyleix. The funeral took place in November 1987.

Ladywell

Ladywell is a place that we are all familiar with, but if you're like me, I wasn't aware of the history of it until I was recently enlightened by Dick Kennedy from Ralish in Abbeyleix. Ladywell is situated approximately 5km from Abbeyleix, 2km from Ballinakill, on a road between the junction at Watercastle, on the main Abbeyleix to Durrow Road.

Ladywell and Shrine of the Blessed Virgin Mary is in the townland of Castlemarket, in the diocese of Ossory, to which they gave their name - Ladywell. The cult of the holy well was deep rooted in the religious traditions of this part of the country, but Ladywell is the sole survivor of holy wells in this and adjoining parishes. The pilgrimage is celebrated each year on the 15th of August, and the Ladywell Novena commences on August the 31st until September the 8th. During the COVID-19 pandemic, the Novena was held online. The visual scene at Ladywell has been transformed and the devotional scene

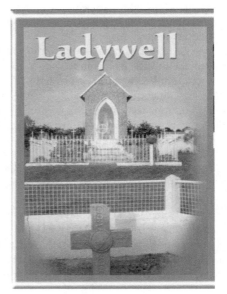

changed completely from days of old. All the principal ceremonies of Catholic worship were found here during the pilgrimage time. Gone are the days where people walked rounds of the well, tied pieces of cloth to the bush and pitched coins or medals into the well.

The pilgrim to Ladywell, seventy years ago and before, followed a grassy path to an open field site marked by an ancient hawthorn or *skeagh* bush which bent over a spring well. There was no shelter at this spot from the wind or rain, people knelt on the damp grass to pray around the holy well. Today the pilgrim arrives to a state-of-the-art site that affords a dry footing and shelter from the elements with space to stand, sit or kneel in relative comfort. The transformation of this site has been brought about over three quarters of a century by an energetic committee supported by clergy and lay people and encouraged by the ever-increasing numbers who have come to pray. The curious and interested will want an explanation of this phenomenon.

What are the origins of Ladywell?

Ladywell is one of the holy wells of Ireland, the devotions at which have survived down through the centuries. Thousands of holy wells existed in Ireland and different types of devotions were associated with them. During the reign of Queen Elizabeth I, daughter of King Henry the VIII, the Catholic faith was suppressed throughout Ireland and holy wells came into their own. Patterns began to develop around the Well's feast day. The most popular of these drew crowds of people from far and near, some coming for prayer and penance, others for enjoyment.

Ladywell is a continuation of the Rosconnell pilgrimage, the origins of which are lost in the mists of time. The first record of this comes from the year 1731 in the report of the Protestant Bishop of Ossory (Tennyson) on Rosconnell Church. In the 1870s, Reverend Patrick Neary was curate in Ballyouskill. He was interested in local history and was a member of Ossory Archaeological Society. In the 1870s, Reverend Neary recorded people still alive who remembered the pattern held at Rosconnell Church. They recalled seeing the fields around the church filled with tents of all kinds during the octave of the assumption of the Blessed Virgin Mary.

The holy well at that time appears to have been in Rosconnell Glebe just across the river from the church. It was known both as Ladywell and the Lodge Well. In the late 1790s, when religious and political tensions rose, the Protestant rector of Rosconnell, Reverend Chamberlain Walker, had the well on his glebe filled up. Tradition had it that a new well appeared at the present day Ladywell, however the possibility cannot be ruled out that both wells co-existed. A feature of holy wells in olden times was that pilgrims came, many from afar, bare footed and fasting to do their rounds or stations at the well and return home in the same spirit. This followed ancient penitential custom. Not everyone who came looked for penance. The pattern was a strange mixture of fun and piety. Most of those who came did so to enjoy themselves and see the 'fun of the fair.' There was eating drinking, singing, dancing, gambling, and the inevitable fighting. Even in the worst of Penal times, the church condemned the conduct at holy wells but could do little about it.

At the beginning of the nineteenth century, Penal laws declined. The Catholic Church had reasserted itself with churches or chapels in almost every parish. The bishops and clergy called for them to be the focal points of Catholic worship. The holy wells with their attendant patterns were to be abandoned. In Ossory almost every parish had at least one pattern. Ballyragget Parish had four - Rosconnell, Kilmenenan, Attanagh, and Finan. The last two named had been suppressed or abandoned long ago. A general clamp down on patterns and visitations to holy wells took place in Ossory around the year 1810, ending the great gatherings at the time in Ladywell.

How did Ladywell survive?
Its location on the border of two dioceses saved it. A ban on attendance at holy wells in Kildare and Leighlin did not exist so the people from Ballinakill and adjoining parishes in the diocese felt free to continue their devotions here. It is therefore thanks to the people of those places that Ladywell was kept alive during the greater part of the nineteenth century. It's interesting to note that on the 15th of August 1880, large crowds attended Ladywell to attend the patterns at the holy well. Authorities drafted in two hundred police officers, one hundred from Queen's County and one hundred from County Kilkenny to prevent possible disturbances.

The attendance continued to grow not only on the 15th of August feast but during its octave to the 8th of September. In 1928, Robert Stephenson became CC in Ballyouskill. A resolute and determined man, he took full stock of Ladywell. Some things about the holy well did not meet his approval. He took a dim view of the ancient hawthorn bush bedecked with scraps of cloth which still bent over the well, it was however to survive him. He also took exception to the fact that the place was a regular rendezvous for courting couples and there was evidence of misconduct by others also. Fr Stephenson was aware that there was an established genuine devotion to the mother of God and that many who came to this lonesome spot did so in a true spirit of prayer. Members of the first Ladywell committee formed in 1929 were from Castlemarket - Bill Mc Gree, Kiernan White, Bill Kilbride, Joe Mc Evoy, Molly Kilbride (later Mrs Ryan) Till Bergin, (Mrs Gough). The first treasure held this position for forty years, later succeeded by Jack Mc Donald who dedicated himself to the task until his demise.

On the 15th of August 1940, Reverend Fr William Kerwick CC recited the first ever public rosary at Ladywell. At this time the surrounding farm, owned by Mr Daniel Kennedy of Abbeyleix, recommended that provision be made for the holy well. He was required by the Irish Land Commission for division among the farmers of the area. Fr Kerwick led the committee in their application for a plot of land around the holy well. They proved successful in this and with Fr Drea, Kiernan White and Joe Mc Evoy as trustees. The enclosure with the well became the property of the committee on the 22nd of October 1948. At the same time, rights of way to the plot from the public roads were granted.

From this time onwards, the rosary was said in public on the 15th of August. The Ballypickas, later Ballyroan, band continues to be in attendance. Their rendering of music for hymns became an essential part of the service. A choir, whose members are from Ballyragget parish, Ballinakill and surrounding areas, led by Joan O' Gorman contributes in a special way to the ceremonies. In the early days, horse, pony and donkey traps and carts, and of course the bicycle, brought pilgrims from afar. People walked round the well, saying a decade of the rosary on their beads in one spot, then moving to another to say another to say the next and so on. Every year the attendance grew larger with people coming from further afield as time went on. The largest attendance so far has been a little over 4,000 people that attended on the 15th of August a few years ago. With the 1950s came the motor car and the fading out of the horse and donkey transport. This development brought with it parking problems. Nothing would have been achieved in this way were it not for the generosity of the two landowners on either side of the well area. Every year, William Butler and Edward Barry opened their gates wide for the full term of the Ladywell pilgrimage.

In 1953, the area surrounding the well was levelled and the drain from it piped and filled. The ancient hawthorn bush was removed at this time. All this work was carried out by voluntary labour. Collection boxes were put up and pilgrims coming in greater numbers meant that the committee were in a stronger financial position and were able to carry out much needed improvements on the site at Ladywell. The work of building the shrine commenced at this time with Ballinakill with contractor Paddy Carroll in charge. With the money collected, a statue of the Blessed Virgin was purchased and erected on Ladywell day, the 15th of August 1954 (Marion Year). The statue was blessed on that day. The artistic railing was made by Joe Mc Cabe from Abbeyleix. Peg White and Ita Brannigan were added to the committee to look after the flowers. From this day on, doing the stations and walking around the well had died out.

Up until the 1960s, the well was fenced only by a sod or clay bank which was broken and unsightly. Fr Thomas Bowden, appointed curate in 1957, organised the entire district and with the help of this voluntary labour, the committee set to work again removing the old bank and replacing it with the present walls and fence which now enclose the area. Electric lighting was installed replacing batteries previously used for illumination. Shelter was provided for the elderly and invalids. When Reverend Joseph Galavan became curate, the first enlargement of the shelter took place. Improved seating also became available. These seats came from the old church in Grogan, Errill.

A new era of devotions at Ladywell commenced in 2001 with the introduction of the novena for the last nine days of the pilgrimage, consisting of public rosary benediction and a guest speaker each evening. In 1983, the field containing about 3 acres was purchased by the committee. The field was adjacent to the holy well, and during the next couple of years the field was levelled for car parking. The sanitary faculties were provided in 1995 and further improvements made to the general area. In 2007, Noel and Patricia Burke of Abbeyleix donated half an acre of land to the Ladywell committee for extra car park space. The account of the early development of the Ladywell site might have been lost had it not been for the memory and commitment of the late Bill Mc Gree which was written about in his personal memoir in 1983, three years before his death. Bill was a member of the first Ladywell committee formed in 1929. Dermot Dorgan & Julie Dorgan, along with others were instrumental in keeping the history of Ladywell at the forefront of our memories.

It's so important to keep the history of our Towns, our County, and our Country alive, and pass it on to the generations to come.

An Old-Timer's Memories of Abbeyleix

Looking Back

Looking back from 1983, Abbeyleix itself has greatly changed since my childhood years. New Row for instance, that's the Mountrath Road now, and it was a very busy part of Town. It had a harness maker, a shoemaker, a blacksmith, a tailor, and a metal foundry. They're all gone now. Living on the road too were carpenters, stonemasons, and bakers. Seven bakeries also operated in the town. Now there's just one bakery here. Names over nearly all the shops have changed. Gone too is the little stream that flowed down the Ballinakill Road, then down along the Main Street to the bottom of the town. It was a feature of the Town at the time.

Rowan trees and Limes

In the 1940s, the County Council saw the stream as a traffic hazard and put it underground. That's when the rowan trees were planted along the footpath. The lime trees on the opposite side of the street must be nearly as old as the Town itself. You will always find plenty of trees in and around estate towns like Abbeyleix. The same can be said of big houses, the houses of 'the gentry' as they used to be called. I can remember people named Sutcliffe living in Balladine House, and further out the Mountrath Road, Green-mount belonged to a man named Milley. The crossroad at Ballytarsna is known as Mille's cross. A big landowner named Foster lived in Tunduff House. On the Ballinakill Road, Glenban was Orme's. Allworth House, a family by the name of Swan's, lived there. Thornberry House was Waldron's. On the Ballyroan Road, a Colonel Campbell lived in Oatlands and Rathmoyle House belonged to people named Singleton.

Twenty-five on the Tombstone

Getting back to the old times, who would be content nowadays to spend their Sundays playing a penny 25? Long ago, not a Sunday would pass without a game of cards in Jim Hughes's work shed on the Ballinakill Road. Jim was a monumental sculptor, a good one, and headstones are still evident in the old Clonkeen and Shanakill graveyards today as well as many others. Jim lived where Mick Grant operated a Blacksmiths Forge during the 1960s. Many a rubber was played on a headstone that he would be putting on someone's grave a week or two later. There were no soft tricks going when you were playing against the likes of 'The Rooth' Mack, Tim Bergin, Joe Strahan, Stephen Moore, 'The Gary Doyle', or any of the others. It used to be said that if you were good enough to play on the stone you were qualified to play anywhere. Jim Hughes married a woman named Margaret Doheny in Ballinakill in November 1906. They had two daughters, one of which was named Kathleen, an Abbeyleix librarian born in 1913. Jim's wife Margaret died in 1917 from TB age 39 years. Jim died in May at his home on the Ballinakill road in 1951. He was born in 1871 to a national schoolteacher from Timahoe, Stradbally. There used to be a toss school up there on the Ballinakill road on Sundays too. Of course, at that time, to get a drink on a Sunday you had to make a bona fide traveller of yourself by going to Ballyroan!

The Longest Lawsuit

Abbeyleix claims a direct link with the longest lawsuit in history. It concerned the endowments to the Preston School. It seems that they were not always judiciously managed by the School's Trustees. The issue commenced in 1734 and was not concluded until 1834. Abuses connected with the endowments were given a very full hearing in the Irish Parliament, the House of Lords and before the Royal Commission of 1807-1812. Preston School, the first-ever post primary school in Co. Laois, was originally established in Ballyroan in 1686 by a Dublin Alderman named Joshua Preston. In 1896, the school was transferred to Abbeyleix and established in what were formerly known as the Assembly Rooms. There it became one of the first ever co-educational post primary establishments. The school closed in 1966.

De Profundis

Another old custom that has gone completely was the saying of the *De Profundis* in Latin at funerals, written by Oscar Wilde. Jack Kirwan of Oldtown, William Delaney, who had a drapery shop in the Square, Jim Crennan, and Jack Duff of Balladine were great De Profundis reciters in their day. They would always be there to say the Latin prayer when the coffined corpse would be put on the two chairs outside the house. They would walk at the head of the funeral saying it over and over again all the way to the Chapel.

More people died at home at that time than in hospital, and when the distance wasn't too far the coffin was carried by relays of six men using strips of white 'calico', a plain-woven textile made from unbleached cotton. Jack Duff was given a nickname from his De Profundis saying. The older people of the time called him 'Davitt' because with his beard resembled the great Land Leaguer. The younger generation, never short of a nickname for anyone, always referred to him as 'Oremus'. Latin meaning, 'Let us pray.' Jack was a great flute player and a grand singer. Jack was born in 1857 and died in 1929 aged 72 years.

Yarns and Characters

Somehow people were more light-hearted in the old days. There was always some bit of 'gallery' going on. Abbeyleix had some great characters - 'Pewcy' Mc Hugh, George Mills, Mickey Fogarty, Bill Haslam, Jimmy Mc Hugh, Ned Brazil, Chris Cosgrove. No shortage of yarns and 'quick ones' from these lads back then. Mary Cruite another great character of her time, owned a little farm in Ballytarsna where she lived alone. Mary loved to prank and wind up all the lads. When the first AI man came to live around Abbeyleix, Mary asked him to come to her farm.

When he arrived, she said, "Are you the man that's going to put my cow in calf?"

"Yes, I am," he replied.

"Well," said Mary, "the cow is in the shed and there's a nail in the door to hang your trousers on."

Carpet Factory in Abbeyleix

The girls here made the luxurious cream and white carpets for the ill-fated Titanic in 1912. The carpet factory, known as Bramley's Motor Works, closed after the outbreak of World War I. Standing on the left is, Miss Brodrick, supervisor. The Abbeyleix girls in the group include the sisters Nell and Bridge Morris, Lil and Biddy Hurley, Julia and Kate Cosgrove, Sarah Clooney, Annie Fitzpatrick, Ena Cushen, and Nan Fogarty. Among the hundreds of people who perished in the Titanic disaster was an Abbeyleix man William Henry Gillespie who bought his ticket in Patrick Ryan's shop, also known as Moran's. He belonged to a family who owned what was then known as the 'Coffee Shop' where Benny Murray had his shop premises.

Music & Dancing

Anything goes for music and dancing nowadays as well. God be with the times when Quinn's Band played at the dances in the Town Hall. The Quinn's lived down in Sweetview and were a very musical family. Later, I enjoyed the music of the Bannon's' Band from Portlaoise, the Ormonde Follies from Kilkenny and the Muinebeag Melody Makers. Music was music in those days and dancing was dancing!

Abbeyleix is not as busy as it used to be

The monthly pig fairs brought a lot of people into town, so did the big Saturday markets. The Railway station, now closed, was a very busy place. You could set your clock to Tom Emerson, nicknamed the 'Boots' at Morrissey's Hotel at the top of the town, going down to meet the commercial travellers. Very few people go out walking anymore. You would see people strolling on all the roads in years gone by. Coleman's Road and 'The Lord's Walk' were great places for courting' couples, but the young fellows all have motor cars now! Times have changed in Abbeyleix.

Lal Deegan

James 'Lal' Deegan was an Abbeyleix man described as being the oldest correspondent that worked for the Nationalist newspaper in their centenary year 1983. Lal wrote about his memories while growing up in Abbeyleix in the early 1900s. Lal had some brilliant stories to tell, about what he saw and heard during those years growing up here. He travelled on the Abbeyleix annual pilgrimage to Lourdes for quite a few years, organised by Paddy Mulhall, where he would entertain the people that travelled with good conversation and brilliant stories that he could tell. Lal can be seen in a video with some great old characters from Abbeyleix in 1983.

Lal lived at upper Main Street. He was a gifted tailor and a correspondent for the Nationalist newspaper. Lal was one of three correspondents from Abbeyleix that provided a great service to the people of our town and surrounding areas, who wrote a column on a weekly basis, keeping everyone informed about what was going on in the locality. This was a time before everyone had a Television or a Mobile phone.

Kevin Higgins was another man that wrote for the Nationalist newspaper and Christy Phelan from New Row, a gifted man with words, was also a correspondent for the Leinster Express. Lal recalled his memories of growing up in Abbeyleix by writing in the Nationalists centenary edition of the newspaper in 1983.

Lal, as he was known to all of us, was born in 1916 and unfortunately died two years after he published his memories of growing up in Abbeyleix in 1985.

Market House

Abbeyleix Market House, or the town hall as it was known to the local community, was built by John, 2nd Viscount De Vesci in 1836. Renovated in 1906, the building became the focal point for almost everything that went on in our town after that. Market Day was held on a Saturday and was largely responsible for drawing huge numbers of people to the town. People arrived in their pony and carts, donkeys, bicycles, and even 'shanks mare.' Abbeyleix was the place to be on a Saturday or the third Monday of every month when the pig fair was held. Abbeyleix was almost a victim of its own success, in that all the women went about doing their shopping during the day while most of the men spent their time in Morrissey's pub and others drinking a tipple or two. The local clergy began to get worried at what they were witnessing on these two particulars days in the month, so they approached a local businessman to open a coffee shop so that the people would have some other kind of beverage to drink instead of beer.

Theatre

Throughout the 1900's, the Town Hall was used for lots of activities including concerts, dancing, and plays. The Abbeyleix Brass Band of 1902 had a dramatic class who performed in the Town Hall during this time. The Abbeyleix GAA or St Lazerian's Drama Society were under the guidance of Liz Lalor and Lal Deegan. In the 1940s, many plays and concerts were produced and performed here as well as in all the nearby Towns. They entered various drama competitions all over the country. At times their greatest competition came from a second drama group which had been formed in town under the auspices of Macra na Feirme with the Mc Donnells, Rita, Gertie, and Benny as the leading lights in this case. Both societies carried on the great tradition of drama and acting which had always been present in the town, for many years.

The GAA club performed the old Irish plays like *Pike O' Callaghan, Lord Edward, Father Murphy, Con the Seachrawn* and *the Bailiff of Ballyfoyle*. Mick Cummins, Mick Molloy, Nicholas Harding, Bill Carthy, and Fanny Kelly were among the actors. Ina  Mc Grath from the Ballinakill Road was singled out as being a brilliant actor. Other people that represented St Lazerian's Drama group in the early 1950s were M Foley, Lal Deegan, Harry Roe, Joe O' Brien, Frank Burke, P Bergin, A Egan, Rita O' Gorman, PJ Lalor, P Moore and Liz Lalor. A younger generation of aspiring actors and actresses also represented the local GAA club in January 1967 when they performed a three-act comedy play, *An Angel Without a Halo*, by S Burke, produced by Larry Kavanagh. The cast included, Martin Lalor, Billy Phelan, Gerry Kelly, Paddy 'Fob' Hill, Billy 'Sabu' Whelan, Joe Mills, Breda Fennelly, A Mc Donald and Mary Phelan.

Mc Master & Others

Mark Wynne had a great company back in the 1920s and Eddie Mack's was another that came to town regularly in those days. Bert Duval and Dave Llewellyn were leading actors of the time, and Dave, a Welshman, was a powerful singer as well. There was also a company led by Mickey O' Shea, his son Herman, the Dobells, and the Baileys. Popular plays were *East Lynn*, and *Murder in the Red Barn*. In more recent times, the town had regular visits from Alec de Gabriel's Shannon Players and Louis d' Alton's famous company. Anew Mc Master's Shakespearean Players also visited. Mc Master always said that the Abbeyleix audiences were the most critical and appreciative!

Maybe he said the same everywhere, but he and all the others gave the town a great stage education. The Abbeyleix people got an opportunity to see some famous actors. Anew Mc Master was an Anglo-Irish stage actor who toured Ireland and Britain for nearly 45 years up until 1959. Born in 1891, he died in 1962.

The Big Protest in Town

The people of the town had great excitement the time of the big protest against the Vic Loving show because the girls in the show were showing too much leg. 'The do Gooders' in the town organised men to protest when the girls would appear on stage. The men attended the show on the second or third night, when the girls came out on stage the men stood up to protest and walked out. It was said at the time that some of the men stood up to get a better look! The show then went to Rathdowney after Abbeyleix to perform their show. A lot of the Abbeyleix 'Do Gooders' that protested earlier in the week were seen sitting in the front row at that show. I suppose it's like the Cole Porter Lyric:

'In olden day's a glimpse of stocking,
Was looked upon as something shocking,
Now heaven knows anything goes.'

Another Abbeyleix Performer

During the early 1950s, a highly talented young Abbeyleix girl embarked on a career which was to earn her and her hometown worldwide recognition in her own sphere. Maura Bonham later to become Mrs Shanahan decided to share her own wonderful talent with the young people of the town and started her own Irish Dancing School, named Scoil Rinnce Bonnean. Almost immediately, Maura and her pupils made a profound impression on the world of Irish music and dance and together with one of her music pupils, Jimmy Hartford, set the exceptionally high standards to which others would aspire. From small beginnings, Maura Shanahan's School of Music and Dance developed and grew, as would be seen later, to virtually encompass the world. Some of the talented girls that were there at the beginning were, Helen Bonham, Bernadine Rice, Christina Kelly, Margaret O' Connor, Barbara Carroll, Lillian Lalor, and Anne Harding.

Entertainment and Dance

Prior to the 31st of December 1961, when there was no such thing as television, mobile phones, Instagram, or even Snap chat, people had to entertain themselves in any way they could. They had to rely on the radio, newspapers, posters that would appear in the town, even commercial travellers that passed through and passed on information to the locals and so kept themselves up to date with what was going on in the world. Just after the end of the war in 1918, cinemas began to pop up around Ireland and indeed Laois as well. Just before Christmas 1923, a new cinema opened in Abbeyleix. Thomas Shakespeare, who ran the Abbeyleix venue, within a few months of commencing his role, had left to take up a position with a more prominent picture house, but was universally praised for doing so much for the town in such a short space of time. It wasn't until 1933, that cinema goers in Mountrath were first in Laois to be treated to sound and vision, a completely new experience for cinema patrons.

The coliseum in Abbeyleix owned by John Egan was a very popular place to go for your entertainment at that time. The first film shown here was the *Four Feathers*, a British film released in 1939.

End of the Cinema

The Coliseum Cinema in Abbeyleix situated on the Mountrath road was leased from 1943 and put up for sale by its owner John Egan in 1966 along with the Coliseum in Mountrath. This was five years after television had first come to Ireland and was seen as progress. New technology if you like and a new source of entertainment for the people. The television was largely to blame for the demise of the cinema in all the rural towns at that time. The cinema was purchased by Bernard Murray and renamed the Milo Cinema in 1967 and operated until the early 1970s until the doors were shut for the last time. It had a 500-seat capacity and was equipped with an imperial sound system.

Macra Na Feirme Was Born

Digging the foundations for the Macra Hall began in 1958. The first to put a spade in the ground was George Galbraith and Bride Reilly. Several young farmers backed a proposal by Sean Reilly to form an Abbeyleix branch of Macra Na Feirme and so it began. Mr Tom Casey became the first President of the branch. Prominent members of those early years were the Reilly brothers, the Cole brothers, Joe Cass, Brian Lucas, and Dick Palmer among others. William Conway was the chairman for fourteen years. Sean Reilly was secretary for eighteen years before becoming President of the branch. The branch began fundraising so that they could build a hall. They raised 5,000 pounds and built the Macra Hall in New Row on the Mountrath road, a marvellous achievement at the time. The Irish Showbands scene had started in the 1950s and became very popular with all the young people in the town, so much so that they travelled to other towns to dance to the top bands.

The completion of the Mara Hall was much welcomed by all the young people in the area, especially since the teenagers, and some not so young could now go and dance to some of the biggest showbands in the country. The showbands continued to play in venues throughout the country right up until the mid-1980s. Several Abbeyleix showbands were formed at that time. One in 1960 called 'The Mighty Rhythm Kings' namely, John Kelly, Dick Kennedy, Paddy Walsh, Tom Cooney, Peter Rogers, Lolly Kavanagh, Jimmy Byrne, and Danny Brennan. They were a very popular band at the time and played support for the likes of Jim Reeves, The Batchelors, Chubby Checker, Hank Loughlin, and others when they toured this country. They played support for Jim Reeves in May 1963 in the Crystal Ballroom in Kiltormer. In 1963, another successful Showband band was formed in Abbeyleix called the Sailors.

Meaney's Antique Shop

Meaney's Antique shop underwent a real transformation of its shop front thanks to some of the local people in our town. The shop front of the antique shop became quite dishevelled over the past number of years because the Meaney brothers, Danny and Pete, that  were running the business fell into poor health and are currently in residence in a nursing home. The building is now visually attractive, especially in a quaint or charming way, full of character. The property has a unique architectural style and design that makes it stand out from the rest. Abbeyleix, a Heritage town, will be quite proud to show off this shop now in any forthcoming tidy towns competition, and hopefully will earn the town a few extra points in any forthcoming competition!

The shop is situated on the Main Street just to the north of the Ballinakill road and directly opposite Benny's pub another landmark in the town of Abbeyleix. Danny and Pete Meaney purchased the shop, petrol pumps, and storage shed at the rear, excluding the garage at the back which had already been divided off by a wall. Benny Murray sold it to them around 1990. The brothers changed the business model from that of the previous owner. They changed it to an antique and furniture business and opened it in 1991 and continued to operate it in that fashion. Pete who had already been in a nursing home for a few years, left the running of the business to Danny who continued to do so until the middle of March 2020 with the beginning of the Covid-19 pandemic.

Murrays Garage

Bernard 'Benny' Murray was born and reared in Fermanagh in the North of Ireland. He teamed up with his twin brother Michael and went into the construction business. Both brothers were building properties in south Dublin, before he retired and headed off to purchase a property in Abbeyleix. He purchased the property that was being operated as a garage, shop, and petrol pumps from Felix Mc Coy. Felix inherited this garage from his uncle Nicholas Harding who already owned another garage shop and petrol pumps that was beside the old Post Office on Upper Main Street. It seems that there was a fire in this garage in the late 1920s resulting in the garage being closed and Nicholas moving to the house above the shop and petrol pumps that became known as Murray's.

Benny Murray purchased this property in 1955 along with the garage that was at the back of the property. It wasn't long before he had a thriving business. The people at this time began to retire their horses, ponies, donkeys, and carts and moved into the new era by purchasing a car, especially the people that could afford to. Benny had a Ford car dealership, which gained him widespread respect based on a perception of his achievements and the quality of the vehicles he was selling. He employed as many as fourteen people at any one time which was very beneficial not only to the people that worked there but also to Abbeyleix town in general as well. Any new car that came out manufactured by Ford was immediately purchased by Benny, brought down, and put on display on his forecourt for all to see. He had a great advantage in that his showroom was beside the shop facing the Main Street so all the people travelling through the town on the main Dublin to Cork Road could see the cars that he had on display. I can remember when there was a lot more room for people to park their vehicles around the square in the town, people could be seen standing around in groups at Murrays showroom looking at and admiring the latest model of car on show. Benny had built his own private residence on the Ballinakill road almost opposite the entrance to Rathmoyle road.

Mick Delaney

Mick Delaney, also known as 'The Hopper', remembers taking up the position as shop attendant in 1967 when he was only 13 years of age. He saw many employees come and go throughout his time working there. Mike had a brilliant personality and was responsible for attracting lots of young people to congregate in and around the shop front. When Benny Murray would arrive outside his shop driving the latest model of car that he had at the time, all the young people would scatter from all over the place before Benny would arrive in and shout at them to get out of the shop!

Mick remembers the two old Ms Parker ladies that lived in the residence over the shop front. When it came close to 10pm in the evening, Ms Parker would bang on the floor with her stick indicating that it was time to close for the night. The two Ms Parkers lived in the upstairs part of the premises, back when it was owned by Felix Mc Coy. They had a lease, or a right to stay there until their demise. In the early 1960s, Benny Murray purchased the Esso filling station just on the outskirts of the town of Durrow on the Abbeyleix road. This proved to be a very worthwhile venture because it was situated on the busy main Dublin-Cork Road. John Joe Bonham, one of Benny Murrays employees from Abbeyleix, ran the filling station for him. Mick Delaney spent a lot of time doing relief work there as well. In the mid-1970s, Benny sold this premise. He soon got tired of having to drive to Durrow to collect Mick in the late evening when the filling station closed for the night. Mick was still underage at that stage and not allowed to hold a licence to drive himself. When Mick retired from Murray's garage, he later went on to become a postman in Durrow. He is currently enjoying his retirement, just like a lot of us.

1966

In 1966, John Egan from Portlaoise put the cinema in the town up for sale. Benny Murray decided to expand his business, so he bought it and reopened the cinema in 1967 and renamed it the 'Milo Cinema.' Television had first been introduced into Ireland six years earlier in 1961 and was largely to blame for the demise of the cinema in rural towns.

The Milo cinema continued to operate up until the early 1970s when the doors shut for the last time. People came from all over the surrounding areas to visit the cinema for their entertainment and were disappointed with the news of its closure. These people would have grown up with the cinema all their life and it being high up on their list of places to go on a weekend night in winter or summer. Benny sold on the cinema to a company that called themselves 'Leatherettes' and they specialised in the manufacturing of Jeans at the time.

Beginning of the End

Mick Delaney was the last employee to leave Benny Murrays employment in 1985. From 1984 to 1985, Abbeyleix was undergoing the construction of the new sewage system, which the Laois County Council had embarked upon. Benny was doing very little business because of the road works in the town. He tried to keep the shop open for a while until it proved too difficult for him. The garage that he owned at the back of the shop already ceased to exist and faded away by the early 1980s. Benny Murray left his home and his business shortly after that and headed back to Fermanagh in the North of Ireland to live. By 1990, Benny suffered huge changes to his health. Diagnosed with Alzheimer's, Benny decided to sell the shop storage shed and petrol pumps to Danny and Pete Meaney. A dividing wall already been built just to the rear of the shop, leaving only the garage still in Benny Murrays possession.

Murrays Garage Final Chapter

A local businessman, Martin Bonham, had an interest in opening a new business in the town around 1990. He had great difficulty in tracking down and contacting Benny Murray until finally Martin was able to put a proposition to Benny in his own house on the Ballinakill road in 1992. Benny was more than happy to accept the offer and so he sold the garage then to Martin. The garage had been derelict for over 10 years at that point. Martin had to reapply for planning permission to resume the use of the garage. This process took over one year to secure. Martin operated his garage business successfully up to 2021. He currently is investing his time and money in another business venture, on this same site. We the people of Abbeyleix would like to wish him his wife Irene and family, the best of luck with their endeavours in the future.

End of an ERA
An auction was held in Harding's Hotel Abbeyleix in June 2000 where Benny Murray's family home on the Ballinakill road was sold by Benny's twin brother Michael and so ending the business interests of Benny Murray in the town of Abbeyleix. Benny's shop and garage was the hub of Abbeyleix town during our time growing up here in the 1950s, 1960s and 1970s. This was the place where all the young people at the time would congregate and discuss the past, present, and indeed our future as well. This premises has been steeped in history for over 120 years in our town.

Coffee Palace
William Henry Gillispie's parents, Richard and Eliza Gillispie, came to Abbeyleix from Carlow in 1884 where Richard was a staff sergeant in the British army. They were a Church of Ireland family and lived in house number 9 in Abbeyleix Demesne, where Richard worked for the Abbeyleix Estate Company as an agent. In 1901, William was described as a grocer's clerk and was still living with his family in house 9 in the Abbeyleix Estate. On Christmas day 1908, Richard died and was buried in the Church of Ireland graveyard. Eliza moved

with her family up to the premises that later became known as Murray's garage in Market Square. Eliza opened a coffee shop there and named it 'Coffee Palace.' William, who had been born in Carlow in 1880, was now 28 years old. He was working as a clerk in the carpet factory.

William Henry Gillispie purchased his ticket for the Titanic in Patrick Ryan's shop on Main Street Abbeyleix, later to become known as Moran's shop. Patrick Ryan was an agent for the *White Star Line* at the time, who were the owners of the Titanic. William purchased his ticket for £13, his destination was Harwood Street Vancouver, British Colombia, Canada. William boarded the Titanic in Southampton first, then on to Queenstown on the 10th of April 1912 as a second-class passenger. He was one of only a handful of Irish passengers not travelling third class. William's brother Daniel lived in Manhattan in the USA, but the family had not had contact with him since around 1906.

The Titanic sank on the 15th of April 1912 and sadly, William's body was never recovered from the disaster. The ship sank in the North Atlantic Ocean just off the coast of Newfoundland near Canada. A headstone that had been erected for his father Richard in St Michaels Church of Ireland graveyard had William's name placed on it. William Henry Gillespie's mother received compensation from the Titanic disaster fund for the loss of her son. Eliza continued with the running of the coffee shop up until her death on the 10th of January 1914. In a strange twist of faith, William's brother Daniel living in New York set about trying to contact his family back in Abbeyleix. He later stated that he had not contacted his family in 20 years. He believed his brother William was working in Dublin as a clerk. He only learned of the fate of his mother and William from the Irish police force. Daniel who had worked as a painter in Brooklyn, was never married. He died on the 15th of August 1929 aged 47.

Change of Ownership
In 1914, after the death of Eliza, the Coffee Palace premises changed ownership. It was purchased by Nicholas Harding, an uncle of Felix Mc Coy, who inherited the premises at a later

time. The name over the door was the 'Refreshment Rooms,' although it was called the Coffee Palace by the Gillespie family, when they owned it.

Mrs Campion

When Time Catches Up

In 2022, Mrs Helen Campion decided to call it a day after almost 50 years in business in this town. Helen operated the business known as Laois Cleaners on the Main Street since 1972. Her other business, H & M Fashions, she operated since 1992 when the old Barbers Shop came into her possession after Ned Hinchin passed away. I can't help feeling a little sad when I recall just how quickly time has passed since Helen first opened her business premises. I've come to the realization that time is catching up on all of us. Helen provided a great service to the people of this town and beyond, one that all the people of this town have been very grateful for.

Where It All Started

Helen Campion (nee Ryan) hailed from Racecourse, Cashel near Rockwell College in Co Tipperary. She is the daughter of John and Mary Ryan, both natives of Cashel. An interesting fact about Helen is that her grandfather Jack Ryan and indeed her granduncle Mike Ryan both played international rugby for Ireland. They made their international debut for Ireland on the

6th of February 1897 when they beat England by 13–9 at Lansdowne Road. Mike played for Ireland on seventeen occasions, while Jack played in fourteen matches for his country. Both brothers played in all three matches in 1899 when Ireland won the triple crown, beating Wales in the Cardiff arms Park in the final match. The match was played on the 18h of March. The score was Wales 0 Ireland 3.

Lifelong interest in Horses

Helen had a passion for horses which came from her grandfather Jack. Not only was he a farmer, but he also bred horses. He famously bred a horse named 'Tipperary Tim' that went on to win the Aintree Grand national in 1928. An amateur jockey by the name of William Dutton heard a friend call out to him just before the start of the race, "Billy boy you'll only win if all the others fall." And they did. Tipperary Tim was one of only 2 horses still standing at the end of the race, winning at odds of 100-1. Jack reputedly had a £5 bet on the horse, netting him a considerable profit. One of Jacks relatives jokingly said to him, "Not a bad result for a horse that was only fed on hay and turnips."

Jack sold off his farm shortly after that and headed off to the USA along with his family, only to return some months later a widower and teamed up with the one son that had stayed at home, also named Jack. The son, Jack, was later to become Helen's father. The popularity, sporting ability, and versatility of the Ryan brothers, in the days before the GAA ban on playing foreign sports, resulted in an unusual incidence of sporting ecumenism when the Tipperary County board of the GAA presented them with an illuminated address celebrating their role in the Irish rugby team's 1899 success. Jack died on the

24th of October 1937 and is buried in the beautiful village of Rosegreen near Cashel in Co Tipperary.

Mike Ryan and Eamon De Valera were very good friends, probably because of them playing rugby on the same team when they played for Rockwell college in Tipperary. Eamon De Valera taught Mathematics and Physics at Rockwell in 1903 and 1904. De Valera said that his day's in Rockwell were the happiest in his life. The Ryan's were his dearest friends. Eamon De Valera wrote a letter to Mike Ryan when he was in Kilmainham Jail after the 1916 Easter Rising, awaiting what he thought would be his own execution.

He said, "Farewell old friend, you are in my thoughts," signed E. De Valera. That letter today is in the National Museum of Ireland. Eamon De Valera went on to serve two terms as President of Ireland from 1959 to 1973. He died on the 29th of August 1975.

Mike Ryan, Helen's granduncle, was saving hay in a field with a horse-drawn rake on his farm in Racecourse, Cashel on the 19th of August 1947 when both himself and the horse that he was working with were killed instantly by lightning. They were standing close to a ditch that incidentally was also badly scorched by the same lightning strike. One of the lasting effects on Helen when she heard about that accident has been an absolute fear of thunder and lightning and has stayed with her to this day. Mike, along with his brother Jack, was also buried in Rosegreen cemetery.

Helen makes her own Way in Life
Helen was born in 1940. After she finished national school in her local town, she went to the secondary school in the Ursuline in Thurles in Tipperary. A Catholic convent school founded in 1787 and run by the nuns. Helen recalls that after her education in this school, she became a fluent Irish speaker because of having to speak the language on a continuous basis. When she continued her further education in college, she recalls finding it difficult to write compositions or essays in the English language due to spending so much of her time speaking the Irish language. She soon found a way around this problem though,

by writing the compositions or essays in Irish, and then translating them back into English and that worked for her.

Helen's First Move

Helen's career started when she joined the commercial bank known as the  National Bank before it had been taken over by the Bank of Ireland. She operated from the branch in Eccles Street in Dublin where she spent 10 years of her life working. Helen soon progressed to working as a travelling cashier for the bank, where she covered vast areas of the country. Helen received the biggest fright of her life in the summer of 1969 when she worked in Derry. Between the 12th and the 16th of August that year, the beginning of political and sectarian violence in Northern Ireland began. This was seen as the beginning of the thirty-year conflict known as 'the Troubles.' Helen was in a property in Derry where the first firebomb was thrown. Helen soon realized that this job wasn't for her, so she packed her bags and headed back home to Racecourse, Cashel in County Tipperary where she felt safe.

A New Beginning

In 1972, Helen purchased the property that was known as Mrs Rose Deegan's sweet shop on Lower Main Street. Rose was formerly Rose Kavanagh from Colt Ballyroan. Some of you may remember that her own daughter, also named Rose, was married to Paddy Gorman, who had a butcher's shop at the end of Main Street in the town. As it happens this sweet shop was once owned by Mrs O' Toole prior to Rose Deegan and was used as a tearoom to feed the volunteers that worked on the construction of the Local GAA Park known as Jelly's Pit. The volunteers were fed with tea and sandwiches in this property during what was called in 1924. Helen soon set about turning it into a dry-cleaning service and named it 'Laois Cleaners.'

Helen already served her time working in Mack Cleaners who were based in Parnell Street in Clonmel, Co

The big Push   *April 1924.*

Tipperary. They were a professional laundry and dry-cleaning service. This is where she picked up all the skills of the trade. Mack Cleaners was operated by Noel Mc Namara, the father of the well-known sports reporter Clare Mc Namara with RTE. He died in April 2019.

Moving On

Helen soon turned her own business venture into a very successful one, when she secured quite a few big contracts from the likes of the Irish Prison service, namely Beladd Park in Portlaoise and the Abbeyleix convent. The Midland Health Board gave her the contract for St Fintan's Hospital. She also secured other

lucrative ones as well. There was quite a few Prison Officers that lived in Abbeyleix and in the surrounding areas of the town at the time, and they were required to keep their uniforms clean and tidy, and so used this service as well. This was a very busy year for Helen because she also found time to change her name from Helen Ryan to Helen Campion when she married Jimmy Campion, a farmer who was also from Abbeyleix. Helen later went on to have a baby girl and named her Mary after her own Mother. After the Barber Ned Hinchin passed away in 1992, Helen opened the business known as ' Fashions' where she went on to operate this business very successfully also.

Helen's Employees
Helen had consciousness hard working people that worked for her in the business over the years. Francis Fennelly is one such person that needs to be singled out as being one of the longest serving members of her staff over those years. Francis continues to check in on Helen every day now that she is in her retirement years. Other people that were also part of her team were Brendan O' Loughlin from Portlaoise, Sean O' Neill from Spink, and Statia Mc Donald from New Row.

The Red Velvet Curtains
Sean O' Neill first began working for Helen in the dry-cleaning service, after he finished working as a barman in Michael Ryan's Happy land in the square of Abbeyleix around 1973. Sean recalls only being there a few days when a woman came into the shop with a pair of big heavy red velvet curtains. The woman asked if it was possible to have them ready for her for the following evening as she was expecting a wedding party in

to have some photographs taken. Helen assured the woman that they would be ready in time for her.

Later that morning she received a phone call and told Sean that she had to go away on business for the day. Sean assured her that everything was under control and told her that he would look after everything. When Helen was gone, Sean put the red velvet curtains into the washing machine. Not sure how to set the machine correctly, he turned it on to boil just to make sure that the curtains would be nice and clean. When the washing machine finally finished, he took out the curtains and placed them in the dryer, turning it up to full heat for two hours. When the bell went off on the dryer, Sean decided to give it another spin just to make sure the curtains would be good and dry. When the dryer finished this time, he opened the door and what he saw was something that resembled a large red football. Sean, panicked at this point, decided to take a day off sick the next day leaving Helen to sort out the mess. Sean doesn't recall getting a bonus for his efforts for that day!

It didn't take Sean long to learn the trade after he used too much of a chemical known as 'Perc', or Perchloroethylene, a solvent used to remove stains on garments. He used this chemical on stained clothes on this occasion when he oversaw the shop for the day. He recalls leaving the shop after he finished work, resembling somebody that was after drinking about 10 pints of beer. Sean recalls waking up the following morning with a big hang over. After he had almost learned how the dry-cleaning business operated, Sean decided to leave and take up painting and found that he was much more suited to it! He did return on occasion to paint the shop for Helen.

(Pictured: Sean O'Neill)

A Trousers for the Wedding

One of the funniest stories that Helen can recall happening to her in the business was when an old farmer that lived close to Abbeyleix came into her one day. He said to Helen, "I have to go to a wedding on Saturday." He had a brown bag with him. He pulled out what could only be described as something that resembled some trousers. It was in such a state that Helen was not sure what colour it was when she was writing out the docket for him.

He said to her, "I want you to promise me that nothing will happen to my trousers. Will it be safe here? This is the only spare trousers that I have and I'm not buying another one."

Helen answered, "I'll give it a good washing and do my best to get the stains out of it, the trousers will be in safe hands."

This was a Wednesday morning and Helen knew that the trousers needed a few trips in the washing machine to have any effect. The old man headed out of the shop in his overalls and wellington boots, feeling reassured that his trousers would be ready for the wedding. Just before closing time that same day, the old man returned and asked about his trouser.

"Everything will be fine, don't worry about a thing," said Helen and so off he went. The following two days, the old man came into the shop on five separate occasions to check on his trousers. When he arrived again, Helen told him the trousers were almost ready.

"Well, the blessings of God on you Mam," he said.

Helen put the trousers up on the counter in front of him and asked, "What do you think of that?"

The old man looked in a stunned silence for a moment before he said, "That's not my trousers, you must be making a mistake."

"There is no mistake, that is your trousers, this pair of trousers was in the washing machine for three washes. We also had to use a chemical on it to try and get the stains out of it as well."

He thought about it for a little while and said, "These trousers won't fit me. Do you have a room where I can try it on? The wedding is in the morning."

"You can use the room at the back. Go and try on the trousers, just lock the door behind you."

The old man was in the dressing room for a while and Helen wondered why he took so long. Suddenly, she heard the door opening. The old man stuck his head out through the door and shouted out, "Jaysus Mam, the f*cking trousers fits me." I can't repeat what Helen said after that!

The Noresiders Athletic Club

The Noresiders Athletic Club was founded in the Summer of 1942 by Harry Mercer. He came to live in the Barracks, as it was known, 'a house near Shiels' in lower Boley on the Shanahoe side of Poorman's Bridge. Sadly, it is no longer there. The Noresiders were a strong club which included athletes from Abbeyleix, Durrow, Castletown, Raheen and Shanahoe. Luckily at the time, athletics was doing well in Laois and prizes for sports were very reasonable.

Noresiders Club

The big men of the Noresiders club were the local Curate at the time in Raheen Rev. Joseph Keogh (RIP) and Harry Mercer, who later moved to live in England. The club was in existence from 1942 up until 1952. The President of the club was the late Fr Keogh, Harry Mercer was secretary and the late Fintan Delaney was Treasurer.

Athletes

The Noresiders produced some outstanding athletes. During those ten years of the club, a record number of prizes were won and not forgetting the cross-country teams who were unbeaten for six years. Willie Delaney, a Cappanaclough man, entered the

athletic scene at a relatively late stage. At 25 years of age, he started with the club and retired from competition in 1950. His biggest achievement, undoubtedly, was winning the Leinster two-mile championship in 1945. Willie, seen in the photograph, was a top middle-distance and cross-country man. The two athletes that Willie Delaney most admired were the Ballincurry hare, J.J. Barry, and a local man, Richard Palmer.

Dick Lalor-Fitzpatrick and Dick Palmer

Dick Lalor-Fitzpatrick and Dick Palmer were strong and speedy runners. The former has the distinction of still being the holder of the Laois five-mile title which he won in 1944. Since Dick Lalor-Fitzpatrick's victory of that year, this distance has not been included in Laois championship events. In 1945 Dick Palmer ran second to the one and only John Joe Barry in the one-mile open handicap at Cullohill. Palmer was still a youth on the way up the ladder to athletic fame, the top rung of which he later reached with phenomenal success. He was none other than the famous John Joe Barry, the 'Ballincurry hare' as he was known as. Palmer won many cross-country laurels with the Noresiders A.C. during that club's lengthy run of successes in the Junior Championship from 1943 to 1949. Sadly, Dick Palmer along with the other athletes have gone on to their eternal reward.

Dáithí Ó Briclí

In 1979, David Brickley became the principal of Shanahoe primary school. He had a great interest in the people of the area and was also the author of '*Shanahoe: A Rich Area.*' A founder of Shanahoe 'Glór na nGael', Brickley had a great love for the Irish Language and believed that it should be revived. It is due to Brickley's record keeping and historical documenting of the Noresiders Athletic Club that we have this information. His work has made this local history available for the benefit of the generations to follow.

The Noresiders Tug- O- War team in the 1970s
Another branch of the Noresiders club was formed in the 1970s. A group of men formed a very successful Tug-O-War Team that represented Shanahoe in competitions throughout Leinster. The team was made up of strong men from Abbeyleix, Killeaney, and Shanahoe. The team attracted large crowds of people, that came and watched them in competitions especially when they were local, such as the Maytime festival in Abbeyleix. The team had mastered the technique required to become successful at this tough sport. They quite often pulled teams much bigger and heavier than them with ease. They won numerous competitions locally as well as in Wexford and other areas in Leinster. They were coached and managed by the experienced George Thompson from Ballytarsna, Abbeyleix. The team was made up of big strong men such as the men in the photograph.

Front row: Charlie Kirwan, Noel Thompson, Jim Coogan, and Billy Kirwan.
Back row- (Murt) Kirwan, Tom Kirwan, Jack Coogan, Pat Kirwan, Billy Turner, and Mrs Anne Kirwan.

An Abbeyleix Hero

Patrick 'Paddy' O'Hara was somewhat of a hero in his time. O' Hara joined the Old Irish Republican Army during the War of Independence. He decided to do his bit in order to win our freedom from an occupational force that invaded the Country more than 700 years ago. The Irish people had never known real freedom at any time during their lives. It's because of the contribution of men like O'Hara, and indeed the women that had joined the Cumann na mBan at the time, that has allowed us the Irish people to celebrate 100 years of freedom this year.

Medical Hall

Paddy O' Hara qualified as a Chemist and took up residence in the Medical Hall on Main Street Abbeyleix in 1938. He served the community to the highest standards until he retired from the business in 1975 after almost 40 years. Unfortunately, after a short illness, Paddy passed away in 1977. Paddy was born in 1902 in the Stanhope Arms Hotel in Ballinakill, Co. Laois. This lovely building has changed ownership on numerous occasions since and unfortunately has now become derelict. His father, also named Patrick, retired from the Royal Irish Constabulary as a Sergeant and bought the Hotel, where he ran the business as well as raising a large family of 10 children along with his wife Margaret.

Paddy decided to follow his dream. Like two of his older brothers, Paddy decided he wanted to become a Chemist. He travelled to Trim in Co. Meath where he went on to serve his apprenticeship in his brothers Chemist Shop. Passionate about history, particularly the plight of the Irish people, Paddy was aware that there were approximately 20 different rebellions throughout our history during the previous 700 years. These rebellions were carried out in an attempt to free Ireland from being ruled by the British Empire. The most memorable rebellions were the Irish rebellion in 1798 and the Easter Rising of 1916. Paddy thought about it long and hard before deciding to join the IRA and contribute to the cause in his own way, taking the complete opposite pathway in life to that of his own father.

Paddy joined the local unit of the IRA in Trim in late October of 1918 just before the start of the War of Independence which began in January 1919 and lasted until July 1921. This war proved to be the most effective rebellion of all. This war resulted in Ireland finally becoming a Free State. The Anglo-Irish Treaty was signed on the 6th of December 1921 which ended British rule in all but six counties. The Irish Free State was created as a self-governing Dominion on 6th December 1922.

First Assignment

Now officially a member of the IRA, Paddy's first assignment was to carry out an attack on the Bellivor R.I.C. Barracks. He was in the front line along with other IRA volunteers armed with a Webley pistol, but Paddy did not get an opportunity to discharge it. One shot was fired in the Barracks resulting in one policeman being shot dead and the other policemen surrendered to the IRA. The IRA took all the arms and ammunition as they left the scene. These would be used at a later time in the War of Independence.

Second Assignment

Paddy's second assignment was to arrest three men for robbing a house where an elderly man lived alone. The old had man died from his injuries a couple of days after the incident. The

IRA had a strict anti-social behaviour rule in place, in that if the people responsible for wrongdoing in their area were caught, they would be deported to England. Paddy's mission was to guard these three robbers until transport was arranged for them. Paddy kept them prisoner for three days and three nights before deporting them. Paddy was also involved in capturing a gang of thieves caught robbing a country house in Tobertynan, Enfielf, Co. Meath, belonging to the Duc de Stackpool. This gang were deported to England.

In September 1920, Paddy was involved in an attack on the R.I.C. Barracks in Trim which they burned down and took the arms and ammunition from the Barracks. He aided the burning of the Tax Office in Kilcooley House in Trim. The tax records held in this office were used by the British to tax locals, but they were all destroyed in the fire. Paddy, along with other volunteers, were responsible for blowing up approximately four bridges in the area that were frequently used by the Black and Tans and the R.I.C. They used these bridges to cross over in their armour cars and carry out raids on people's homes.

Paddy lands in Trouble

In 1921, Paddy lands in trouble, as one of the robbers that he previously arrested and deported to England joined the British Army while he was over there. This soldier's unit was not only sent to Ireland but ended up in Trim where Paddy operated from. The soldier spotted Paddy on the street and reported him to his superiors. The IRA had sympathisers in the new R.I.C. Barracks in Trim where they warned Paddy that his house was going to be raided. Paddy managed to avoid them for about five or six attempts, until they finally managed to catch up with him. Paddy was arrested and brought to Mountjoy before being brought to court and found guilty of imprisoning this soldier and deporting him to England.

Paddy was sentenced to two years penal servitude. He was transferred to Hull prison in Yorkshire in England. While serving his time there breaking stones, a splinter from a stone flew into his eye causing Paddy to lose the sight in that eye for the rest of his life.

Anglo Irish Treaty

When the Anglo-Irish Treaty was signed, Paddy's sentence was commuted to one year. He was released on the 9th of January 1921 and sent back home to Ireland. He was only home a couple of months before the civil war broke out in June 1922. The war lasted until the 24th of May 1923. Paddy was recalled by the IRA and asked to take up active duty again. When he was sent out on his first mission, he found that he was fighting against friends and colleagues with whom he had served. Some of which he had spent time in prison. Paddy decided he had enough, left and took no further part in the civil war after that.

Paddy O' Hara's Service Medals

The following is a description of the medals that was earned by Paddy, a very brave Abbeyleix man during the War of Independence:

1. The Service Medal with Bar, (1917-1921).

    The Bar, inscribed with 'Comac' awarded to members who rendered
    active service.

2. The Truce Commemoration Medal (1921)

    Awarded to Veterans of the War of Independence who were alive on
    11 July 1971

3. The Local Security Medal (1939 – 1945)

    Awarded to persons who served in the L.S.F. during the Emergency.

A few years ago, Paddy's son Gerard set out to find his father's service record from the Military Archives in Cathal Brugha Barracks in Rathfarnam, Co. Dublin. He also met with the Governor of Hull prison in Yorkshire where Paddy had served his time in an effort to try and piece together the complete picture of his father's life. We owe a great deal of gratitude to the men and women like Paddy O' Hara who sacrificed a lot for the parts that they played during the War of Independence, helping to bring about our Nations freedom from over 700 years of occupation by the British. As we celebrate 100 years of freedom now in 2022, spare a thought for all those brave men and women of this country that made the dream come true.

Patrick Begadon

The Black & Tans

The Black and Tans, in Irish 'Dùchrònaigh', were constables recruited into the Royal Irish Constabulary (RIC) as reinforcements during the Irish War of Independence. Recruitment began in Great Britain in January 1920 and approximately 10,000 men enlisted rising to about 14,500 during the conflict. They arrived in Ireland in January in 1920.

Who were the Black & Tans?

The Black and Tans had a reputation for violent indiscipline that could be dangerous to Irish civilians and even other policemen. The role of the RIC as a largely domestic police force with strong community ties had been steadily compromised since 1916 by more aggressive tactics against nationalists and heavier reliance on the military. Diarmuid O' Hegarty, the director of communications for the IRA, left no room for ambiguity when he composed a memorandum that year on what targeting of the RIC should amount to - "The police should be treated as persons who having been adjudged guilty of treason to their country are regarded as unworthy to enjoy any of the privileges or comforts which arise from cordial relations with the public."

Historical Heritage

Patrick Begadon, from Aughmacart, recalls only too well the stories that he was told about the infamous Black and Tans. These stories were told to him by his father, who witnessed the Black and Tans first hand. Aughmacart is a townland in county Laois, situated near Rathdowney, Cullahill and Durrow. Around 1156, Aughmacart had a little over 2,200 people living in it. In the mid-12th century, there was a town in this area with a Church and Castle located there. The Church was built around fifteen hundred years ago, in the year 550. This is known as St Tighernagh's Church, Aughmacart. It was built on the site of a thirteenth century Augustinian. Most of the churches in this country were damaged, or destroyed during the reign of Queen Elizabeth I, and the practising of the Catholic faith was prohibited. Priests were persecuted for saying mass. If caught, they were imprisoned and quite a lot of them were executed.

Around the 18th century, several the churches were rebuilt. The church in Aughmacart is still standing proudly here today. The Priory in Aughmacart was in the 43rd year of the reign of Queen Elizabeth granted to Florence Fitzpatrick, Barons of Upper Ossory. All the Fitzpatrick family are buried in an enclosed tomb in the graveyard situated beside the church. The burial vaults at Aughmacart are said to have penetrated far under the building to the north of the Protestant church. Only one vault is now to be seen here, it belongs to the Fitzpatrick's of Coolcashin. This Church of Ireland church and mixed graveyard is close to where the ruin of the castle still stands today. Most of the castles were built in this country between the years 1177 and 1310. This castle in Aughmacart was built around the year 1425, by Mac Gillapatrick, Lord of Ossory. The castle was almost as high and as large as the castle in Cullahill. The castle at Aughmacart collapsed from its foundations in 1850. About 30 feet of the east end of this castle remains visible here today.

The Story Begins
The story begins when Martin Begadon, Patrick's grandfather, who was born in 1851. While Martin attended the local school, he also worked as an Iron moulder. Martin completed his training as an Iron moulder before coming to live in Aughmacart where he set up his own Iron foundry business. He met and married a woman named Mary Conroy and they went on to have 11 children. They settled down and lived in a house that he built beside the stone constructed forge that he had already erected on the site. Martin operated a very successful business here. All the farmers in the area came to him with their horses, ponies, and donkeys for shoes to be fitted. This was the mode of transport for almost everybody at the time. Martin built stables in his yard for the farmers to leave their animals while he shod the horses. The farmers would return in the evening and collect their animals with their shoes fitted.

Martin's Forge was close to the river Gowl, a tributary of the river Erkina and the River Nore. Martin diverted water from the river using hydropower to power the Mill wheel, which he had erected on the outside of the building, adjoining the forge. This river powered a milling machine which was a tool that cut metal as the workpiece is fed against a rotating multipoint cutter. The milling cutter rotated at a very high speed due to the multiple cutting edges. It cut the metal at a fast rate. The machine was able to hold single or multiple cutters at the same time. They also used this system for stone milling work. The local farmers would bring their wheat and corn to them at harvest time to have it milled. The grain was first put into a Hopper which held the grain. Then the damsel shook the grain, so it travelled down through the shoe and into the eye of the upper stone. The Begadon's had a fleet of seven Threshing Sets on the road. These sets went out to thresh the ricks of corn in the farmers haggard's, beginning in September and continued until the following January. They covered areas not only in Laois but the surrounding county's as well. Martin was a gifted tradesman, and that accounted for the fact that he was always busy.

Martin Begadon   *Kieran Begadon*

Martin's Death

Martin died in 1916. Both of his sons, Kieran aged 27, and Martin aged 19, followed in their father's footsteps. Kieran and

Martin took over the running of the business and were equally as efficient as their father before them. Both brothers worked extremely hard keeping all the local farmers happy with the service that they provided for them. In 1920, the Black and Tans were not only in Dublin, but they were also across the country, harassing and intimidating local people. Kieran signed up as a member of the Irish Republican Brotherhood around 1916 while Martin signed up as a member of the Old IRA. At the time, their sister Mary (Dunne) was already a member of Cumann na mBan. Both the brothers were approached by leaders of the Laois branch of the old IRA and were asked to make grenade and bomb casings and road mines.

Making The Grenades
Kieran and Martin began making the grenade and bomb casings for the IRA and storing them on the premises, until they were collected by two Roscrea men named John Maloney and Paddy O' Meara. When the grenade and bomb casings were collected, they were then taken to Tullamore to a chemist named Edward J Quirke where they were filled with explosives and a detonator inserted. The bombs, when primed, were distributed to various IRA brigades and the Flying Columns throughout the region. The Black and Tans began to target the Iron Foundry's at that point, the Begadon's as well as the Mc Hugh foundry in Abbeyleix, and others. Several of the Mc Hugh sons previously served their time and learned the skills of the Iron foundry business in Aughmacart a few years earlier. The Black and Tans were constantly harassing the owners of these foundries. They suspected that the bombs were being made in these foundry's but were unable to find any evidence, despite searching the premises on numerous occasions.

House Search
The Begadon's house was searched more than most, so they built a secret room just off the upstairs bedroom in the house where they hid the bombs. The two men that came to collect them in the event of the Black and Tans coming in without them being forewarned. This happened on a few occasions, when the two men had to quickly get into the secret room in the house, as

did Kieran and Martin. The room had a low set window leading in over the dairy and adjoining the forge. They fashioned a double ceiling and floor into the space. The double ceiling prevented the Tans from discovering the secret hiding place. Their mother was in a bed pushed up against the aperture and the Black and Tans never disturbed a woman in bed especially a widow woman. They were aware that her husband Martin had died in 1916.

The RIC
The Royal Irish Constabulary in the area never ceased harassing the Begadon's. They did not rest until they got both brothers jailed, which they eventually did. Both brothers, along with Jack Mc Evoy from Oldtown in Aughmacart, were eventually caught by the Black and Tans in the Grove which was close to where the three men lived. Kieran was sent to Kilkenny Gaol for 6 months on suspicion of helping the IRA. Martin and Jack Mc Evoy were imprisoned in the Curragh Gaol for a further 6 months. Both brothers accumulated autographs from fellow prisoners that were there at the time. That autograph book is now the property of the National Library of Ireland having been donated by Fr Sean Dunne, a son of Mary who inherited it in 1983. The key which released Eamon de Valera from Lincoln Prison in 1919 was made in Aughmacart. It was brought into the prison in a cake and the key that finally released him had a small triangular file included. There was a blacksmith from Kilkenny also a prisoner there, he filed the key to suit. Eamon de Valera visited the Begadon's house in Aughmacart later along with Dr Comer from Rathdowney who had been involved with the IRA. He was imprisoned in the Curragh for the part he played in the struggle. When the Civil War ended, both brothers were reluctant to speak about their involvement in the troubles. They decided to have 'no hand act or part' or any further political involvement after that.

Final Chapter
Kieran was reputed to have been the brains behind the grenade and bomb making operation. He was eight years older than Martin. In 1964, he died and was buried in Rathdowney. Martin

married a woman called Mary Clancy in 1932 and had 13 children together. Patrick the youngest son, the man who recalled this fascinating story was born in March 1945. Martins' wife Mary died in 1945. Martin died and was buried in Durrow in 1985. Patrick agreed to tell his family's story on video and give a small demonstration of the type of work that he has performed all of his working life in the actual forge owned by the Begadon's. I would like to thank Patrick and his family for giving me the opportunity to document this wonderful piece of history. Patrick has no intention of retiring, so we would like to wish him and his family the best of luck in the years ahead.

Mc Hugh Foundry

In this story, we follow the plight of an old Abbeyleix family
that lived in our town 100 years ago. The efforts that they made
as a family to help in their own way to bring about freedom
from an occupying force that existed here in our town, our
county, and our country during their lifetime until everything
changed on the 6th of December 1921, is a story that is not
commonly known. Ireland was England's first colony. We lived
as part of the British Empire for over 700 years. The Normans
first conquered Ireland in 1169 and aside from a brief decade of
independence during the 1640s, Ireland formed an integral part
of the English imperial system, until 1922 and the foundation of
a modern state.

A Forgotten Business
There is a now a forgotten business that operated in Abbeyleix
in the nineteenth century and continued into the early 20th
century. John Mc Hugh, also known as John Mc Cue, along
with his brother Michael were both gifted tradesmen. They

originally came from Watercastle in Abbeyleix before moving to Rathdowney. They eventually returned and set up a new business in Abbeyleix where they worked as Iron Founders. John lived in number 15 New Row Abbeyleix and operated his business from the Forge built at the back of his house. Twenty-eight houses stood in New Row at that time. They remained in place until about 1911 when several of them were demolished. Knocking down old buildings means the loss of historical and architectural heritage, to me personally, and it is not something that I'm particularly keen on. The Mc Hugh's' trade was in iron foundry work. They worked with cast iron, brass, aluminium, repaired all classes of machinery, and fitted new parts. Hay bogies, ring rollers, and plough fittings were their speciality. They also made manholes and storm drain covers that were used along the Main Street of our town. The iron cross that the Mc Hugh's made to mark the graves of loved ones are still evident in Abbeyleix, Athy, and various other graveyards today.

The Mc Hugh's were never short of work. Local farmers and businesses, such as John Baggot's business on Lower Main Street Abbeyleix, relied on them to supply the machinery. John Baggot was a general merchant that sold machinery purchased from the Mc Hugh's at the time. Every piece of iron work that the Mc Hugh's made in their forge had the name John Mc Hugh stamped on it. Ploughs that they made were purchased by farmers that lived around Abbeyleix and from all over the midlands as well. For a short time though, with some of the machinery that they made, they had changed the spelling of their name to 'Mc Cue'. Some of the Mc Hugh family that emigrated to England continued to spell their surname as Mc Cue. Matt Mc Hugh, John's eldest son, was an assistant foundry specialist learning his trade initially from Thomas Phelan who had his own Foundry business in Aughmacart. In 1901, Matt was spelling his name as Mc Cue at the time.

The Mc Hugh's were an industrious family who travelled to the local matches. When the Abbeyleix GAA football and hurling teams played their games in Coyle's field up in Ballymaddock, directly behind Squiz Cranny's house, they would travel with their horse and cart loaded with sweets, apples, oranges, drinks and the like and sell them at half time and the conclusion of the match. On certain days during the month, they would travel around the area with their horse and cart collecting old iron that the local farmers had dispensed with, bring it back to the forge, melt it down, and re-use it.

It seems that the Mc Hugh's were in business in the town as far back as 1884. An anchor plate that they made with the name John Mc Hugh from Abbeyleix, and the date stamped on it can be seen clearly fixed on the wall of the coach house constructed adjacent to Millbrook House Abbeyleix. John Collison from Abbeyleix, the current owner of Millbrook House, is having the house restored to its former glory and will hopefully look as well as it once did when completed. This beautiful house was built in the year 1884 and certainly coincides with what John Mc Hugh has stamped on the anchor plate.

John married a woman named Bridget Byrne and they had eight children - seven boys and one girl. John was by all accounts a witty man and was known to be quick witted with a reply. Apparently, John was fond of a drink or two and didn't always pay his rent on time. An agent for the De Vesci estate, H. Fitzherbert, was out collecting rent for the property's one day when he met John up the Town.

Fitzherbert said to John, "Mr Mc Hugh, do you know that there are a number of people looking for your House?"

John replied, "Be God Sir, I wouldn't worry about it. Sure, I do be often looking for it myself." And that was the end of that conversation!

Times were tough during the early 1900s. John's eldest son Matt had taken up the trade as an iron founder, along with his younger brother, Thomas. When 1914 came along, two of John's sons joined the British army and went off to fight in the First World War. They remained in the army after the war was over and lived in Manchester and Leeds until they both died in the early 1940s. Some of the other children moved to England to seek their fortune just like so many of our own family members did. In 1919, John found the pressure of life just too much, and retired from work. He lost his wife Bridget at 49 years of age and his brother Michael also died in the same year.

Both Michael and John were extremely close all their lives as a result of them not only being brothers but working together in the same foundry. Soon after, John fell into poor health and struggled in life until he died in 1925. John, Michael, and their wives, are buried in the same large plot in the local graveyard in Abbeyleix. Two separate iron crosses were erected by the Mc Hugh Bros in memory of their parents, Aunt and Uncle.

War of Independence

In January 1919, the Irish war of Independence began and continued until July 1921. It affected the entire country and Abbeyleix was no exception. The Mc Hugh's began making grenade and bomb casings for the IRA at this time and were severely harassed by the occupying British forces for doing so. The British forces suspected that all the foundry's in the Country were making the grenade and bomb casings which was probably true and were then being used against them. When the bomb casings were constructed in Abbeyleix, they were then taken away to a different location filled with explosives, where a detonator was inserted. They were primed and distributed to the various IRA brigades as well as the famous North Tipperary Flying Columns. The bombs were used against the British forces by the IRA during the War of Independence. It's amazing, giving the number of times that the Mc Hugh premises was raided by the Black and Tans, they were never able to find any evidence of them at the Forge.

Although John Mc Hugh had fallen into bad health and retired from actively working in the foundry himself, he continued to impart his vast knowledge of foundry work to two of his sons, Joe and James. Joe and James perfected their craft and learned how to make the grenade and bomb casings from the Begadon brothers, Kieran and Martin, from Aughmacart. Kieran and Martin already signed up as members of the IRB and the IRA respectively around 1916. When the Begadons had constructed their grenade and bomb casings, which were large enough to blow up an armoured car, they were collected by two men from Roscrea named John Maloney and Paddy O' Meara. The two men delivered them to a chemist in Tullamore by the name of Edward J Quirk in Co Offaly where they were primed.

A detonator inserted and then delivered to the various IRA brigades and Flying Columns.

Joe Mc Hugh continued making the grenade and bomb casings where he spent three weeks away at any one time hiding out on the mountains of North Tipperary. When he was taken to the North Tipperary Mountains by the IRA, he was blindfolded, and the same process happened on his return to Abbeyleix. While constructing the bombs and grenades for the famous North Tipperary Flying Column, he would only return to Abbeyleix so as not to arouse suspicion in case his presence was missed by the Black and Tans. Joe Mc Hugh married Margaret 'Madge' Fitzpatrick, from Clonin Mountrath on the 14th of April 1941, and they had four children. Joe met Madge in the late 1930s while he worked in the foundry in Mountrath owned by the Carthy brothers, Sean and Nouze. Joe Mc Hugh confided in his wife some 20 years after the War of Independence that he actively made bomb and grenades casings for the IRA during the war. He took no part in the Irish civil war which began after that.

In 1949, Joe Mc Hugh emigrated to Manchester, England, until he died of a head injury in 1967. His wife Madge died in 1996. She almost reached 80 years of age. Unfortunately, this man like so many others never enjoyed the freedom that he fought for. Joe Mc Hugh, as well as all the other heroes that fought for Irish freedom that we have today, should have been recognised for the sacrifices that they made. When the War of Independence ended on the 11th of July 1921, it was accepted by the Mc Hugh family. They accepted that the war was over at the time and played no further part in the struggle after that.

James Mc Hugh, on the other hand, continued his involvement through the Civil War which began on the 27th of June 1922. He was one of 21 Irregulars that was arrested at the sandpit near Coole, Raheen on the 28th of July 1922. This was the Tunduff ambush. James, along with the 20 other Irregulars, were arrested and imprisoned in Portlaoise Prison until they were eventually sent to the Curragh to continue serving their time. The Irregulars were eventually released from the Curragh detention centre in 1924.

Matthew and Thomas

Matthew and Thomas Mc Hugh were experienced foundry workers. They left Abbeyleix and went to Athy, Co. Kildare, and then Donegal, where they set up two separate iron foundry businesses in 1911. One in Meeting Lane and the other in Janeville Lane. The Mc Hugh's operated a successful foundry business in Athy making manholes and storm drain covers. These are still evident today.

Matthew Mc Hugh died in May 1942, and his wife Elizabeth in 1958. Thomas died in 1960. Unfortunately, that was the end of the Mc Hugh's' association with the foundry business.

Finally

The Mc Hugh's from Abbeyleix were a respected family. They provided a great service to the local farmers and businesses alike and they played a pivotal role in the Irish struggle for freedom during the War of Independence. The family deserve to be recognised, and never forgotten for the service that they provided in our town at the time.

Rathmoyle

Rathmoyle House

Having lived most of my life in Rathmoyle, I always felt proud and privileged to have lived among some of the best neighbours anyone could hope to have. Childhood friends I made back then have stood the test of time. Unfortunately, some have passed on now, reminding me of just how short our lives really are. Growing up I sometimes wondered about the name of the place where I lived and why it was named that. I wasn't aware of any 'rath' in the area, so I set about finding out the answer to my question.

  Abbeyleix, as we know, was a planned estate town built on the new Dublin-Clonmel coach road on higher ground to the southeast. When the town was first moved from Old Town to its present location, it was known as New Rathmoyle, and for several years as New Abbeyleix, or simply New Town. Eventually settling on the name Abbeyleix. The historian Sir Charles Coote described the Town in 1801, 'as a market town.' The town extended across two townlands, Rathmoyle and

Knocknamoe, with up to 100 houses initially. Among the first to take a lease on a plot in the new town was the Morrissey family who came from Freshford, Co. Kilkenny. They built a small, thatched house on the Main Street and opened a grocery shop, thereby starting what was to become one of the oldest and most prominent businesses in the town.

Rathmoyle House, seen here in the photo, built around 1760, is a beautiful residence situated in the heart of the Abbeyleix 18-hole Golf course. The house was once used as a private school for girls, run by Mrs Robert Wilde in the early 1900s. It is believed that the girls were happy there and their education was enhanced by the beautiful setting in which they found themselves in. This house is currently occupied by the popular Reilly family. Rathmoyle, or Rath meaning Ringfort, and Moyle or Maolain was the reason the name was given. The ringfort was evident in the 1840 Ordinance Survey map. It is reported that the dimensions of this ringfort were believed to be of a high status in Ireland and is likely that such a ringfort represented one of the earliest settlements of distinction within the Abbeyleix area. Ringforts usually date back to the iron age, around 500 BC, and the early Christian period of the 5th century. The existence of Ringforts largely went out of favour with the arrival of the Anglo-Normans in the 12th century. Unfortunately, this historic site was bulldozed in 1953, uncovering human remains that lay within. The ringfort was situated just outside the boundaries of the golf club and Rathmoyle House. It is such a pity, and a crying shame, that this historic site wasn't preserved for the people of our Town, our County, and our Country.

The first three-bedroom cottage that was built in Rathmoyle was constructed in 1905. It was built for a man named Philly Cass. Dan Cass, a man that owned and operated a business close to the hospital in the town, was a builder that had ten men working for him. Dan owned the land known as Rathmoyle, so he decided to build houses on it. He began building in 1905 and built thirty cottages with three bedrooms on the land over a period of five years priced at £75 pounds each. The houses had one acre of land attached to them. The second house he built was where Mick Phelan, also known as a baker, lived. When Dan finished building the houses on that road where it connected with the Ballyroan road, he returned to Philly Cass's house and continued building down towards the town. The fourth house down where James Brennan and his family now live was built in 1908.

Dan Cass continued building towards the town where the original Rathmoyle house can be seen. He began building houses on the opposite side of the road facing in the direction of the ones he had already built. When he reached the site where he built the house for Richard Lodge, opposite James Brennan's house, it was 1910. Dan Cass had only one more house to build after that and it was built for Mary and Jack Mc Hugh. The Rathmoyle cottages were completed by the end of 1910, and these houses appeared in the census in 1911 Incidentally, Dan Cass died in the year 1911. Twelve new houses were built by Laois County Council in 1948 and these houses became known as New Rathmoyle.

Jampots

Growing up in Rathmoyle was so much fun back then. Many young people lived in both the new and the old Rathmoyle. Times were so much different back then compared to nowadays. Parents allowed their children out to play on their days off school and during the holiday season. When you left the house in the morning, off you went to meet up with your friends, to play cowboys, build ranches, go to the park and play hurling, and usually end up getting into all sorts of mischief, all within the rules of course. The girls did their own thing as well, playing house, performing drama plays and then charge the boy's a penny to go and see them perform their acts. They held singing competitions and everything else in between. Parents never worried about their children back then, they would always return sometime during the day when they either got hungry or tired. *(L-R) Nancy Pratt, Kitty Anderson, Mary Sheeran*

As far as I can remember, everyone from Rathmoyle were proud to be called 'Jampots', girls included, and is still the case today. My own house, where I live now, has an inscribed stone built into the front gable with the word 'Jampot' written on it. The boys from the town and other areas were only too happy to refer to everybody in Rathmoyle as Jampots. And we were never offended. How Rathmoyle actually got the name was because a lane way that joins the old Rathmoyle with the new Rathmoyle road was used in competitions. Bow and arrow and catapult were very popular back then with all the young boys. Basically, jampots were put up on Mickey Clooney's gate post situated halfway down the lane. These were used as targets by all the boys taking part in the competitions using their catapult. It was only a matter of time before the lane was covered in broken glass.

Quite often you would begin to run out of jampots, and the question was always asked if you had much more jam left in the pot in your house. Every young boy in the place ate as much bread and jam as they could so that they could bring the jar over to the lane when they were empty and use them for catapult practice. The lane was soon christened Jampot Lane, named by the local boys themselves and the name stuck ever since. Not many people owned cars at the time, so the area was always free from traffic. Bicycles were the order of the day, and this was the mode of transport used by most people at the time. This was the only road in the country that I'm aware of where people had to carry their own bicycles from one end of the road to the other because of the broken glass scattered everywhere!

Finally

Now that I am well into my pension aged years, I sit here and reflect over the life and times that I grew up in Rathmoyle and the wonderful town of Abbeyleix. I remember all the great people that have lived in Rathmoyle at the time, all the friends that I made and just think how lucky I was to have grown up here. Sadly, times have changed now. I no longer live in Rathmoyle but in a different location, still in Abbeyleix. I think of the wonderful times that I had and indeed some of the sad times as well. Most of the people that I knew that lived there, and lots of the friends that I made back then, have all passed on now making way for a whole new generation of people that now live in Rathmoyle. I feel sad also when I think back, and admit that it was a mistake now, not to have documented and recorded some of the great stories that I heard and have now forgotten. As now I conclude my memories of having lived in Rathmoyle, I'm reminded of a poem I learned as a small boy when I attended the North School in Abbeyleix, entitled, 'The Old Brown Horse.' This poem was written by W. F. Holmes, and I have never forgotten since.

The Old Brown Horse

The old brown horse looks over the fence
in a weary sort of way
He seems to be saying to all who pass:
"Well, folks I've had my day-
I'm simply watching the world go by,
And nobody seems to mind,
As they're dashing past in their motorcars,
A horse who is lame and half-blind."

The old brown horse has a shaggy coat,
But once he was young and trim,
And he used to trot through the woods and lanes,
With the man who was fond of him,

But his master rides in a motorcar,
And it makes him feel quite sad
When he thinks of the day's that used to be,
And of all the times they had

Sometimes a friendly soul will stop
Near the fence, where the tired old head
Rests wearily on the topmost bar,
And a friendly word is said
Then the old brown horse gives a little sigh
As he feels the kindly touch
Of a hand on his mane or his shaggy coat,
And he doesn't mind so much

So, if you pass by the field one day,
Just stop for a word or two
With the old brown horse who was once as young
And as full of life as you
He'll love the touch of your soft young hand,
And I know he'll seem to say
"Oh, thank you, friend, for the kindly thought
For a horse who has had his day."

(Pictured: Shay Fennelly)

Parish Of Abbeyleix

History of Abbeyleix

The land belonging to the Abbey of Leix was estimated to be 820 acres, as stated in a document contained in the Chief Remembrance's Office. This grant was subsequently assigned to Sir John De Vesci, ancestor of the present family, deriving the title, Lord De Vesci. On the map of Clonkeen, prepared by Sir William Petty, among its townland denominations we find, Abbeyleix, Clohoge, Boyley, Clonkeen, Grealagh bog, Ballymullen, Ralish, Rathmoyle, Ballytarsna, Tunduff, and Blackhill. In 1657, Abbeyleix was a vicarage. The rectory being an inappropriate meaning at the time, it was granted as an ecclesiastical benefice. A ruin of the Cistercian Abbey could not be found towards the end of the eighteenth century. However, tradition has left some reminiscences of its site. For the inhabitants of the modern town of Abbeyleix have a belief, that the house that belonged to Lord De Vesci's fine modern mansion, within an extensive and well wooded demesne, occupies the exact position of the ancient Abbey in the garden attached. It is said some of its former walls and memorial ruins are still preserved. However, this has never been confirmed. In the graveyard attached to the site, and beyond its present precincts, numerous human remains have been unearthed. There was a tradition among the old inhabitants, that portions of the former Abbey were retained in the wall that encloses a burial ground in which stands a deserted Protestant church now closed, and contiguous to the mansion that belonged to Lord De Vesci.

Melaghlan O' Moore's Tomb

Melaghlan, Mac Owney O' Moore, had this tomb made in 1502. He has been correctly rendered Malacias into Melaghlan, the proper anglicized form of the old chief's name as his son is called Conyll mc Mallaghlen in the inquisitions. The inscription running around the edges of this tomb is broken off at two of the corners, so that at present it reads, translated into the

English language - "Here lyeth William O' Kelly who got me made in the year 1530. Pray for him." The inscription is "William O Tunny" Translated "William O' Tunny made me." Unfortunately, this historic site is not open to the public to view on the Estate at the moment.

The De Vesci Estate

Abbeyleix house, the seat of Viscount De Vesci, was built in 1774. It is quadrangular in shape, four storeys high, and faced with cut stone. The noble demesne comprises over 700 acres, covered with forest trees of indigenous growth and a variety of exotics, where splendid avenues and open spaces do not intervene. Some trees are of enormous proportions, and others are disposed in ornamental groups. In the mid-eighteenth century, the modern town, called at first New Rathmoyle, then New Abbeyleix finally settling on the name Abbeyleix, to distinguish it from the former collection of thatched houses, was laid out by Lord De Vesci. South-west of Old Abbeyleix has fallen into decay. Near it were flourishing flourmills and a woollen factory in the beginning of the 19th century, belonging to a Mr Leach. The fine mansion of Knapton is also to be seen in the vicinity, with several other lovely residences.
The houses of Abbeyleix present a neat appearance on the Main Street. With an ornamental and memorial fountain, erected to the founder Lord De Vesci, in the semi-circular marketplace it is abundantly provided with garden plots attached to each of those dwellings. It was a post and market town that had fairs throughout the year.

The Protestant church was originally built by a loan from the Board of First Fruits, but since that time it has been enlarged and renovated into a beautiful Gothic style. Situated near the Abbeyleix House, it has ornamental grounds surrounding it. On the 3$^{rd of}$ December 1839, Abbeyleix was declared the head of a Poor- Law Union. It had electoral divisions - Abbeyleix, Ballinakill, Timahoe, Ballyroan, Raheen, Castletown, Aghaboe, Killermogh, Coolkerry, Aughmacart, and Durrow. The Workhouse was contracted in Abbeyleix on 16th June 1840. It was completed for £5,850 and £1,050 for fittings and contingencies. The Brigidine nuns were brought to

Abbeyleix at this time. When their convent was built beside the former chapel and on an elevated site in 1843, a boarding school for young ladies was founded. They also conducted the female and Infant National Schools in the town.

The old chapel showing signs of decay was removed, and the present beautiful structure of Irish-Romanesque design was erected on its site by the Very Rev. James Lalor, P.P. The first stone was laid in the year 1893, and the church was speedily completed exteriorly and interiorly in a manner that commanded approbation. The architect was a Mr Haige, and the cost of erection and decoration amounted to about £6,000, including the New Tower to accommodate a grand-toned Bell already procured.

Shark in the Mash

Who remembers the summer of 1985 and the moving statue phenomenon in Ireland? In several parts of the country, statues of the Virgin Mary were reported to move spontaneously.
In Ballinspittle, County Cork in July 1985, two ladies out for a stroll claimed to have seen a roadside statue of the Virgin Mary move spontaneously. Similar occurrences were reported shortly afterwards in Waterford, and around thirty other locations across the country. Thousands gathered at many of the sites, out of curiosity or to gaze in wonder and pray, some hoping to see and believing they would witness the phenomenon themselves. Up to 100,000 people visited the Ballinspittle site alone. The Catholic Church remained highly sceptical, and a bishop declared the whole phenomenon an illusion.

Anthropologist Peter Mulholland argues that the continuing role of Marian apparitions in Irish popular culture reflects the psychological insecurity stemming largely from adverse childhood experiences and a 'concatenation', meaning, linking things together of historical cultural, political, religious, and sociological factors. The Ballinspittle statue was damaged by a gang of hammer-wielding protesters a few months after the first reported sighting of the moving statue. The moving statue phenomenon quickly faded away apart from a few groups who persisted for a few years after the peak of activity of 1985.

The Shark in the Mash

The Mash is an area containing around 300 acres of low-lying land situated close to the river Nore on the outskirts of Abbeyleix town. It's accessed by a narrow lane from a place called Cappinaclough. This road joins up with the Mountrath road, with the Ballytarsna to Shanahoe road, just about four kilometres west of town. For approximately six months of the year, this area of land is submerged in water, and floods right across to the Abbeyleix-Mountrath road at Derrykearn and then flows under the bridge. Gun club members, wild geese, mallard ducks, snipe, and plover, are the only form of life to be found in this area between November and May. The Mash is known as a common and is farmed by a number of different farmers during the summer months. On the 3rd of June 1959, one Wednesday evening, news broke about a sighting that was witnessed by a local boy, named Jim Crennan. He met up with Sam Phelan outside Bergin's pub in the town and explained to him what he saw. He told Sam that he walked down the lane and into the Mash the previous afternoon. This was in the month of June. Jim saw a shark in the Mash.

Jim went down the lane to the Mash to see if the water levels were beginning to recede. It had been a wet spring that year and the water was slow to recede back into the river Nore. He wanted to plan his farming activities along with his brother for the summer months. As soon as Sam heard the news, he made his way up to Lal Deegan who was a local reporter for the Nationalist newspaper. Jim Crennan and Kevin Tyrell saw a Shark in the Mash in an area known as Julia's bowl. It was named as such by the local people, because the river Nore bends around at that point in the shape of a toilet bowl, and the name to which it refers was that of a woman that lived down the lane back in the early 1900s. Her first name was Julia. Jim saw the shark jumping up and diving back down into the lake. He said it was about twelve or fifteen feet long and was black in colour. Lal Deegan travelled to the Mash and interviewed Jim Crennan. Jim told Lal that he hit the Shark with about 30 bullets from a .22 rifle that belonged to his brother, and the bullets only bounced off its back.

Lal wrote a story about the sighting of the Shark in the Mash after he had visited the site himself. The story appeared in the Nationalist newspaper on page 8 of the paper the following Saturday, 6th of June 1959. When the article appeared in the newspaper, it started what could only be described as the California Gold rush of 1848–1855. People began to flock to the Mash hoping to catch a glimpse of the shark for themselves. People headed out there every day, whether it was on shanks mare, or on their bikes and parked them alongside the railings of the houses that were close to the lane. They tied up the bikes with binding twine, short ropes anything they could find basically, to secure them while they headed on down to the Mash. Bobby Taylor a local hackney driver thought all his Christmases had come together at once. Bobby was hired every day to take people out to the site, drop them off and then take back. Bobby collected his clients from outside Bergin's pub and dropped them there as well on the way back. Some of the people went in for a drink after their day out and discussed the story of the shark.

Some people said that they had seen it, while others said they saw nothing. By the time some of the people left the pub, the shark had grown from a reported 12 ft long to about 20 ft, and this of course only encouraged others to travel out to the Mash to see for themselves. The people that said they saw nothing were told that they were looking in the wrong place, and so returned to see if their luck would change. Some said the shark could usually be seen basking out there in the summer sun, right out there in the middle of the lake during the early morning time. You could barely see the back of the shark under the water, just lying there quietly. Jim Crennan, Kevin Tyrell, Fint Brennan and Mary Carroll nee Moore, erected signs along the road directing the people to where the Shark could be seen. The signs read 'Shark this Way.'

This phenomenon lasted for about 3 weeks or so. Some observed something large and black in colour out there in the middle of Julia's bowl, while others could see nothing, especially if it had rained the night before and the water levels had risen. The carcase of an old donkey could be seen close the bank on the lake, only fuelling people's beliefs and their assessment of the situation, therefore determining that the shark must have eaten it. A local farmer that farmed close to the Mash reported that two of his Friesian calves were missing, while another farmer said that two of his dogs were missing too. They all suspected the animals of being eaten by the shark. Kevin Tyrell, now in his 85th year recalls that Doctor Mc Donagh, the Abbeyleix GP arrived out one day, parked his car close to the lane, got out and put on his wellington boots and told Kevin and others that he was going to investigate the sightings of the Shark. Things got very serious later that week when the ISPCA came to town and held a meeting in the local FCA office. They ordered that the shark must be shot without delay. Two members of the FCA arrived from Portlaoise and spoke to the guards about the Shark.

About thirty members of the Gun club were organised to meet at the Mash at 3pm on the Sunday, their job was to shoot the Shark. Jim Crennan, Fint Brennan, Kevin Tyrell, and Mary Carroll asked Lal Deegan the reporter for the Nationalist if it was possible to get a photograph of the shark, so that was organised. When news had spread about what was going to happen on the Sunday, people came from various parts of the county to witness the shooting. A lorry was organised to take several people from Stradbally to the Mash. When the lorry arrived in Ballyroan en route, the people on board decided to avail of the drink laws that were in place in this country on a Sunday at the time. This was a legal loophole from the days of coach travel which stated that if you could prove that you were a Bona fide traveller and lived more than 3 miles from where you were going to partake of alcohol, it was okay to do so. This law meant that you could drink outside of the normal drinking hours. One drink led to another, so this group of enthusiasts never got to complete their journey. It didn't stop some of them telling their wives and family when they returned home later that night, that they had seen the Shark! More than 500 people were counted there on that Sunday. No sighting of the shark was seen, I'm afraid. All the gun men stood down.

Mystery Solved

Three weeks after the first sighting of the Shark, about twenty people travelled to the Mash in a group. They parked their bikes outside the house that was nearest to the lane entrance. It was a Sunday morning. Bobby Taylor and Jackie Bergin dropped off a few people from their hackney cars at the same time. The crowd headed to the Mash. What they saw came as a complete shock to all of them. The water had receded back into the river Nore and all that they could see was a black bonnet of a car sitting up in Julia's bowl. Several of the sightseers were not happy, when the penny finally dropped and they realized that it was all a hoax, they said they were going to look for Jim Crennan and the others. It has been said locally that anyone that went to the Mash to see the Shark, never went to Ballinspittle to see the moving statue. It has also been said that every day is a school day, and you'll learn something new every day!

The Infamous Five
The infamous Five that were involved in concocting this story about the Shark in the Mash were Jim Crennan, Kevin Tyrell, Mary Carroll nee Moore, Fint Brennan, and Seamus Tyrell. The boy's had voted for Mary as the ringleader of their group. Mary was the only girl in her family, she had five brothers and was well able to keep them all under control. They said that they had dragged the black bonnet of the car from Fint Brennan's house all the way across the Mash. They initially thought that they would use it as a raft on the water but found that it wouldn't sail. After they realized that, they went about setting it up in Julia's bowl, pretending that it was a shark. When the children were asked why they did it, their reply was, "we only did it for the laugh."

The Donkey
The same children had been involved in another incident at an earlier time, where a grumpy, contrary old man that lived as a neighbour close to where the children lived had absolutely no time for children. When the children walked past his house on their way to school, if he saw them, he would shout at them, telling them to walk on the other side of the road, or he would

find something to say to them. They could expect the same treatment when they were on the way home as well.

When the children complained to their parents about this old man, they told them to ignore the old man. He was a bit odd, that was all. The children came up with their own plan one Saturday morning. They knew that the old man would be gone into town for his shopping, so they met up at the pump which was their favourite spot. The children always made their plans sitting beside the water pump that supplied water to all the neighbouring houses in the area. It was close to the entrance of the Mash. The children spotted one of the windows in the house was open, and that's where one of them climbed through and opened the front door of the house. The children then took a loan of a farmer's black donkey and brought him up to the front door of the house. The children got behind the donkey and shoved and pulled until they managed to get the donkey through the front door and into the kitchen of the man's house. They locked the door again. They waited for the old man to return.

They had a long wait as the man didn't return for two hours. When the children spotted him returning on the bike, they hid behind a ditch and waited for him to open the front door. The children were watching him as he opened the door. He just stood there and looked in a stunned silence for a moment until he began to scream and shout. The children didn't hang around to see what happened next. When they reached adulthood and reflected on the things that they did as children, they all agreed that they would probably be sent to a detention centre if it were to happen today. They later heard later, that because the donkey had been in the house for so long it had deposited the contents of its breakfast on the kitchen floor.

The Wake

When these children were young, if somebody died that they knew, it was customary for the children to attend the wake as well as the adults. A neighbour of theirs that they had known all their lives, was a friendly old woman, that had lived well into her nineties. This old woman walked the roads every day, whether it was to go into town, or collect potatoes, or turnips from a field that was close to where these children lived. She would walk alongside her donkey and cart where she would go into Abbeyleix town on occasion to do her shopping which was about three miles from her home. This woman was almost completely bent over, and always walked in a stooped over position.

When the woman died, her wake was arranged in her house. Some of the local women that were used to laying out a corpse attended and laid out the body in the bedroom of her home. The local people attended the wake in the house including the children. The children knelt on the floor on the opposite side of the bed, while the prayers were being said. The room was full for the prayer service. While the prayers were being said, the children noticed that there was twine that seemed to be holding down the body of the woman, and it was keeping her in a prone position in the bed. The twine was secured tightly to the floor and could only be seen from underneath the covers that were covering the corpse. One of the children had a penknife, one that he always kept in his trousers pocket. He cut the twine while the adults were engaged in prayer. As soon as he cut the twine the corpse sprung upright from the bed, like a shot out of a gun, resulting in the woman's false teeth flying out of her mouth and across the bedroom floor, frightening the daylights out of everyone in the room! The

children never said that they were responsible for the chaos at the wake.

Shortly after that, the children began to go their own separate ways. One of the families headed off to England to seek their fortune. Kevin Tyrell and Mary Carroll are the only two people left from that group of children. They have met on occasions over the years and recounted the times when they were young. They believe that they were the good old days. Kevin recalls that there was no Television back then, you had to make your own fun and games.

Both Kevin and Mary are now in their eighties, so we would like to thank them for recounting their memories of their childhood and wish them all the best for the future in their retirement years. Kevin currently lives in Manchester, while Mary lives in Knapton close to Abbeyleix town. Not many of us can say that we were as mischievous as these children were back in our day. They certainly were great characters and knew how to entertain themselves.

The Widow's Curse

Growing up in Abbeyleix in the 1950s and 60s, when there was no such thing as television to entertain us, we had to, for the most part, try and entertain ourselves. Sport, such as GAA, and the odd film that we were allowed to watch in the picture house if we were good were how we passed the time. On the 31st of December 1961, when television was first introduced in Ireland, my earliest memory of a television was standing in a crowd outside Noel O'Connors shop at the lower end of the town, located beside Quinn's shop. This was where we gathered to watch the television known as *Telefís Éireann.* Noel O' Connor had the television switched on in the window for all to see.

I believe this was his way of advertising to the public that he sold televisions, and we were only too glad to pass on the word. *Telefís Éireann* first began broadcasting from 7pm in the evening, so that's where you would find us at that time if you were looking for us! The other form of entertainment that we were accustomed to was listening to ghost stories told by the older generation. Stories that would frighten the living daylights out of you. Two such stories have stuck with me – The Widows curse and Pickett in the Pier.

A Widows Curse

Folklore is documenting how people viewed the world around them, and it is not shy when it comes to expressing the rage that was felt against the upper classes. Legends which describe widows 'cursing' their landlord have enjoyed widespread popularity in this country, particularly in the wake of the evictions that spread across the country following the Great Famine. These stories detail the revenge which was reportedly waged upon the landlord who happened to evict a poor widow woman from her home. As the most vulnerable member of society, the widow's power to curse people via ritual imprecation – meaning a spoken curse, and prayer - seemed to stem from her perceived powerlessness at the time. The most common of these rituals involved the widow kneeling down, sometimes in an area of strategic importance. For example, outside the home of the intended target. This act could also be coupled with the widow raising her arms in the air and praying destruction upon the intended targeted person.

The curse could cause ill fortune or bad luck to follow the person and his family for seven generations. A male member of each generation of the family would meet with either a violent death, an untimely death, or some other kind of tragic end to their life, such as their prized land and livestock dying away. If the cursed man planted seed on his land, nothing would grow in its place except brambles and thistles, his potatoes would blacken and decay.

Pickett in the Pier

The story begins in Ballypickas in Abbeyleix. Everyone has heard stories about a haunted house at some stage in their lives, but this is about a haunted stone pier. The story goes back over 200 years, when a family by the name of Gorman's lived in a thatched house situated down a long lane, in a place called Bernard's Grove close to the present-day hurling field in Ballypickas. This stone pier was near to their family home. The pier was built more than 200 hundred years ago without the use of cement or mortar which wasn't available then. This pier still stands today in as good a condition as it was the first day it was built. It was erected beside a right of way which allowed people to travel across from one road to another, linking a road known locally as Blandsforth with Tullore. A very wealthy landlord by the name of Bernard Pickett owned a significant amount of land and property in the area. By all accounts he was a horrible man that looked down on people that he considered to be lower class citizens. People that were poor or downtrodden, and people that had to scrape for a living were nothing in his eyes. Bernard Pickett drove a horse drawn carriage pulled by two of the finest white horses in the land. When Bernard Pickett drove his carriage along the road, if he met someone walking in his direction, he would shout, "Get off the road, and let me pass!"

The people at the time were very afraid of Mr Pickett, so they would jump into the ditch to allow his carriage to pass. Bernard Pickett had at an earlier time evicted a widow from her home. One day, the widow was walking along the right of way at Gorman's house, when she met Bernard Pickett on his carriage.

He shouted, "Get off the road, you old hag, and allow me to pass." The woman refused to move off the road. This enraged Bernard Pickett, so he jumped down from the carriage, took out his whip, and beat the woman until she had almost lost consciousness. He pushed her off the road into the ditch and left her there.

He returned to his carriage and continued along the road. When the widow was able to move, she knelt on the road and placed a curse on Bernard Pickett and his family. The following day he passed by the pier again. His horses reared up and he was thrown from the carriage. He landed on the ground close to the pier where he was trampled to death by his two white horses. News spread quickly about the accident, but the people were overjoyed with the demise of the hated Mr Pickett. Shortly after Bernard Pickett had been buried, the Gorman's were woken from their sleep at midnight with the sound of horses' hoofs trampling around outside at the pier. When they went out to investigate the noise, they could not see or hear anything and returned to their house. Every night at midnight after that, the sound of the horses' hoofs was heard trampling around at the pier. Lots of local people were afraid to pass by the pier after that, especially after dark. The Gorman family found this noise unsettling, so they contacted the local priest who came and witnessed what was happening for himself one night. The priest arranged an exorcism to be performed at the site. When this was performed using holy water and prayer, the spirit was locked inside the pier, and has remained inside the pier to this day. Even though the pier was built in the wrong place for modern day farming, no one would ever dream of having the pier removed. The spirit was contained within the pier and the Gorman's were never troubled again with the sound of the horses' hoofs trampling at midnight.

The older generation of the Gorman family eventually lived out their lives in this house, but to this day nobody has ever lived or set foot in this house again. The ruins of the house are still there plain to be seen today. But is this story just folklore? The story of Bernard Pickett is still told around Abbeyleix and Ballyroan to this day, especially around Halloween time.

The Old Barbers Shop

The old Barber's Shop was operated by one of the truly great old characters of Abbeyleix. His name was Ned Hinchin. Ned was the son of Patrick who hailed from the USA back in the late nineteenth century. He joined the postal service and worked as a postman from the post office in Oldtown, along with my own grandfather Daniel Burke. Patrick was married to a woman named Catherine Duff who was born in 1874. They married in February 1911 and had three sons. James died in 1924 aged 12 years, Patrick J died in 1945 aged 30 years, and Edward 'Ned' was born in 1914. Catherine was the daughter of Edward Duff a farmer that lived in Ballymaddock Abbeyleix.

Ned lived with his parents on the Ballinakill road where he went to school and spent his youth growing up playing lots of different sports along with his friends of which there were many. He represented his town and his school with distinction. Ned was a popular young boy and developed the art of conversation. He had a gift that when he spoke, people would stand and listen. Ned went on to develop a skill that he had a talent for, cutting men's hair. After serving his time to the trade, he went on to open his own business on the Main Street in 1940. Ned's barber shop, complete with a barber's pole displayed over his door, soon became popular with the men in the locality. So much so, that every Friday evening and all-day Saturday his waiting room was full of clients.

When somebody sat in the chair for a haircut, Ned would engage him in conversation and quickly after that everyone in the waiting room would join in the conversation. This was how the people passed on and received information at the time. Saturdays was not a day for young boys to have their hair cut, this day was reserved for the adults when all the adult conversations took place. I'm sure the same applied in the ladies' hairdressers as well.

I remember being told by my parents as a young boy, to go down along with my brother and get my hair cut. This happened every seven or eight weeks or so. I was always told to go to Ned Hinchin for my hair cut even though there was one other Barber in the town namely Edward Lalor. Ed seemed to have his own clients, some of Ed Lalor's clients also went to Neds barber shop for the chats only. When Ned finished cutting my hair, I would say "How much do I owe you for the hair cut Mr Hinchin?" I was always told to refer to adult men as 'Mr.' Ned would answer, "Ah, you are alright son, sure I know your father." Of course, Ned knew that my father and almost all the other men around town would be in to have their hair cut. Some would go into him just for the chat only, and even people without hair were also seen there! As Lal Deegan would say, "Times were simpler and more relaxed back then."

Ned's Golfing Day's
Ned was a keen golfer but could only play on a Wednesday afternoon, when it was a half-day in Abbeyleix at the time, or on a Sunday. Des, his son was a good golfer and encouraged by his father to become the best he could be from an early age. The key component to becoming a good golfer is to start when you're young. Ned later went on to become the Captain of the Abbeyleix golf club in 1966. His Captain's prize was presented to Paddy Breen in the Golf club on the Sunday evening after the results were announced. In later years, Ned played almost all his golf in a group of 4 known affectionately as, 'Dad's Army.' The members of that group were Paddy Kelly from Thornberry, Joe

Higgins from Rathmoyle, and Pierce Shiels from The Rock
Ballyroan.

Golfing in Tramore
The annual golfing trip to Tramore open week was always
eagerly awaited by some of the Abbeyleix golf club members
such as AJ Cole, Dan Murphy, PJ Lalor and his son Joe, Eugene
Fennelly, Ned and Des Hinchin. On one such open week, back
in 1977, the golfers had landed. They discussed tactics for the
weeks golf ahead, chose their partners that they would play with
and so on. Their accommodation for the week was caravans,
parked close to the sea, and more importantly closer to the golf
course. The first day's golf was a foursome's competition, for
non-golfers this means each person would only play every
second shot from Tee to Green. PJ Lalor and his son Joe were
markers for Ned Hinchin and Eugene Fennelly in this
competition. The story is still told today about when they
reached the 8th Hole, Eugene Fennelly drove the ball from the
Tee box. The ball had gone so far up the fairway, that there was
only 130 yards left to go to the green. Ned marched off in front
of the group with his pencil golf bag that would only hold half
the number of clubs that you are allowed to carry. When they
reached their ball, which was about 130 yards from the green,
Paddy and Joe Lalor had made their way up and stood alongside
Eugene and Ned at their ball.

Ned said to Eugene, "Hey Euge, would an 8 iron get
me in there?"

Eugene assessed the situation and said, "No, Ned, I
don't think it will."

"Fair enough so," said Ned, "it'll have to be a 3 wood
so."

Well Paddy Lalor fell down on his knees laughing and
had to be helped up off the ground about 5 minutes later
exhausted. I appreciate that if you're not a golfer you may not
get this joke!

The V -Par Competition
The next day, Des was partnered with his father in a v-par
competition. They had discussed the tactics in the caravan the

night before. They knew that in order to be successful in this competition, they had to get off to good start. Des drove off first and unfortunately went out of bounds. Ned hit his ball straight down the middle, the next shot landed on the green about 30 yards from the pin. A mist had descended over the Tramore golf course during the early morning which had resulted in the greens being very slow. Des said to his father, "Da, you'll have to hit it.". To which he replied, "Don't worry, I'll hit it." Des's father hit the putt so hard, it sailed on past the pin and off the green completely. Needless to say, there was no par got on that hole. Their partners couldn't quite hear the conversation that the men were having when they walked off to the next Tee box.

The Jack Russell
Thursday was the biggest competition of the week. It was the Big Four-Ball, played throughout the whole day. An excitement spread amongst the Abbeyleix golfers in this competition. High hopes were held that some of them would feature in the winner's enclosure that evening. Eugene Fennelly was part of a fourball team which included Ned, who was doing quite well when they got to the 4th Hole. This was a dog leg hole, where golfers were expected to hit the ball so far down the fairway and then to turn right for the next shot. When the four men reached the dog leg, they discussed the fact that there was an old man sitting on a stump of a tree smoking his pipe roughly around where the ball would be landing.

This old man sat just outside the boundary of the course watching the golfers as he had done all the week along with his little Jack Russell. During the week, when golfers would hit their ball, if it landed within 50 yards of the old man, his little dog would run over and pick up the ball. This was happening throughout the week. When Ned was just about to take his shot, his partner warned him about the dog. Ned replied, "By Jaysus Shep, you're not getting this one." Ned, insistent that the dog would not get it, let the ball fly. The ball went so far off course that the dog didn't even have to stand up to get the ball, it landed right beside him. No trophies were won that day I'm afraid. The Abbeyleix golfers enjoyed their golfing trip so much that week that the stories are still being told about it today 44 years after the event.

Neds Final Days
Ned continued playing golf and working in his Barbers shop right up until the 17th of April 1992. My own two sons were the last two people to have had their hair cut by Ned. I sent my sons, Noel and Kevin, down to Ned to get their hair cut that evening. They were aged nine and ten at the time and went to Ned Hinchin that Friday evening. Hindsight is a great thing. At the time, I wondered why it was taking so long to have their hairs cut. Ned's normal closing time was 6 pm and this was already 6.30 pm, after the two boys had been in the Barbers shop since 5.15pm or so. Later, I learned that Ned had felt unwell and had been taken into Portlaoise Hospital where he unfortunately died the next day on Saturday the 18th of April 1992. He truly was a great character. In Abbeyleix golf club, Ned has always been held in high esteem, and quite rightly. The Ned Hinchin Trophy is played for on an annual basis.

The Barbers Pole
Eugene Fennelly, a golfing friend of Ned Hinchin and a former Laois hurler and a low handicap golfer, was overwhelmed when he was offered Neds Barbers pole. Eugene gave the pole to his son Eoghan who has it proudly displayed over his Barbers shop, *Sideline Cuts*, situated on the Main Street in Abbeyleix. The

pole is still in very good condition after having been on display in our town for over 81 years out in all weathers. Another generation to carry on the tradition of cutting hair for this town.

The Boccough Ruadh

Can anyone remember the story of the 'Poormansbridge' in Abbeyleix, and how it came to be named as such? In the year 1757, when travellers would try to cross the River Nore that divided Abbeyleix from Shanahoe, they would cross at the 'Ford' which was a crossing point made up of large flag stone laid across the river like steppingstones. Passing across the river in the summer months did not cause much of a problem to the man or woman that tried to do so. A man by the name of Neale O' Shea, lived with his wife and children in a cabin about a mile away from the crossing point on the river. No other cabins lay nearby. Occasionally, Neale would be called upon to help travellers to cross the river, especially if it was flooded. Neale was very obliging and would do anything to help somebody in distress.

One wild and stormy December night, when the angry foaming water of the agitated river beat against the huge limestone rocks that formed the steppingstones of the ford, Neale's wife thought she heard a cry from someone in distress. She immediately called her husband, who was asleep at the time. Neale put on his coat and headed off down to the ford. He stood for a moment at the ford, in the wind and the rain, and cried out as loudly as he could if anybody was there. A voice called out from the other side of the ford to help them. Neale crossed over, found a man and grabbed him.

He asked him, "Who are you?"

"Whoever I am," the stranger faintly replied, "you are my guardian angel, and it was my good fortune which caused you to come and rescue me from my watery grave."

"Whoever you are," said Neale, "you're coming along with me, and you can shelter in my cabin." So, he carried the weary traveller back to the nice warm fire, where he was given food and a warm bed for the night.

The stranger had only one leg and was on two crutches. He was up early the next morning, preparing to leave, when Neale and his wife told him that he was in no condition to leave. He needed to get better and stronger. The stranger agreed to stay for a few days until he felt better. This man, reputed to have been from Ulster, joined a ship's crew and sailed the seas. On one of his voyages, his boat was attacked by smugglers just off the coast of France. He was shot in the leg, which later had to be amputated. He was fitted with a wooden leg, but because he was of little use and unable to fulfil his duties on board the ship, the captain removed him and left him on the shore in

Wexford Town. He eventually made his way up along the banks of the river Nore from New Ross until he reached the ford where he was rescued by Neale O' Shea. He spent every day sitting on his favourite flag stone at the ford begging from the travellers, of which there were many that passed along the way. He wore a large red woollen nightcap tied tightly under his chin and never took it off, day or night.

It wasn't long before this man became known as the 'Boccough Ruadh', or the 'Red Beggar.'

He sat on that stone, begging every day for 40 years. The stone that he sat on became known as the beggar's stone. When he was dying, he swore he had no money to buy a coffin and did not want anyone to touch his cap. He wanted the cap to be buried with him when he died. When he died in 1794, he was buried in Shannikill graveyard close to the ford where he spent 40 years of his life. They found 300 golden guineas stitched inside his red nightcap, and 100-pound coins hidden under the beggar's stone. The money was used to build the bridge, incorporating the beggar's stone into it. This bridge became known, from that point on as 'Poormansbridge.' Next time you cross over Poormansbridge, spare a thought for the Boccough Ruadh.

Temperance Street

TEMPERANCE STREET

In 1842, Thomas, the 3rd Viscount de Vesci was responsible for an innovative project in the town. He arranged for twenty-three houses to be built in Temperance Street for a section of the community whose needs would otherwise not have been met by any other source. They were built from the proceeds of the profits of the Abbeyleix Loan Fund Society. Thomas's father, the Rt Hon. John Vesci, and 3rd Baron Knapton, was an Anglo-Irish politician and peer. Around 1790, John de Vesci planned and developed the new town of Abbeyleix because the original settlement was subject to flooding from the river Nore. Modern Abbeyleix is one of the oldest planned estate towns in Ireland.

The Temperance Street houses comprising of two blocks of similar styled houses were constructed facing one another and divided by a wide U-shaped roadway. Most houses had their own allotment provided and most of them had a garden. Each row of houses was constructed in a straight line directly behind a two-storey house. One of which is now named Knocknamoe House. One part of this house has an office that is now being used as the Parish centre and another part of the house has an office which caters for the Abbeyleix Parish Development Company.

A two-storey house, directly opposite Knocknamoe, was occupied by the Reilly family when I was a teenager growing up in Abbeyleix. This house was later purchased and lived in by the Bradish family and is still in their possession today. The houses were built in a Gothic style. The whole effect was reminiscent of a medieval Alms house complex. The history of the alms houses stretches back to medieval times when religious orders cared for the poor, originally called hospitals or Bede houses. People who occupied these houses at the time were renting them for a nominal fee charged by the de Vesci family, the same as they did with their tenants during the famine years in the mid-1840s.

A Monument erected in the Market Square Abbeyleix to commemorate the second Viscount de Vesci was constructed and unveiled in 1855. This is a free-standing limestone construction with four lion mask waterspouts. It also features a water trough for horses, used extensively when farmers came to town during fair day's that were held in the town on the third Monday of every month. Farmers also came to town with their horses on Market Day which were held on Saturdays during the early 20th century.

The 1901 Census reveals that there were 59 houses in Temperance Street at the time, housing as many as 219 people, made up of family members and boarders in many cases. This will come as a huge surprise to many people of my generation who were not aware that there were so many houses in Temperance Street during this time. Housing and the lack of accommodation at the time in Abbeyleix was an issue just like it is throughout the Country today.

The census for Temperance Street show that the house numbers had reduced from 59 houses in 1901 to just 23 in 1911. The reason for this was because 36 of the 59 houses that were described as being in Temperance Street in 1901 now had a new address named the Ballinakill Road. It seems that this street had only just been renamed prior to the census of 1911. A total of 88 people lived in the twenty-three houses in Temperance Street in the year 1911.

Maria Mullally Remembers
Maria remembers the time she lived in one of these Alms houses in Temperance Street. Her memories are of the people that lived in them. When Maria was young, the house that is

now known as Knocknamoe house was two houses in one. Facing the road lived Mr and Mrs Talbot, next to them lived a Miss Kelly. In the small cottages, John-Joe Bonham a great character loved by all who knew him lived in the first one. John-Joe worked in Benny Murray's Garage at the time where Benny operated a Main Ford car dealership in the town at the time. Next to John-Joe was Chrissie Burke and her brother Billy. Mrs Mary Burke lived next door. Next to her was Dil Freeman who lived with his mother and looked after the Church and graveyard. Dil was also responsible for the ringing of the Church bell, which included the Angelus at midday and 6pm. The Church bell was also rung for Mass and funerals. When he married his wife and had children, he continued to live in his homeplace.

The house beside Freemans was where Maria lived with her Grandmother Nancy Pratt. Their neighbours next door were Moll Coffey, Jimmy Cass, and Bridget Bonham. On the left-hand side of the street, the house that everyone knows as Bradish's house was also a two-storey house. In the front, and facing the Ballinakill road, was where Tommy Riley lived. Around the other side, Miss Byrne lived. The first small house on that side was lived in by Maria's great grandmother, Elizabeth Brazil and Mary Breen. Tom Warren and Gary Doyle shared the house next door. John 'Gary' Doyle was very witty and was known to be very quick off the mark with an answer when called upon. He was a well-known character in the town of Abbeyleix, almost every adult and teenager alike that lived in the town and its surrounds knew Gary Doyle, and almost all could remember either a story or a saying that he was famous for.

An article appeared in the Nationalist newspaper that said Abbeyleix will never be the same again with John 'Gary' Doyle of Temperance Street had gone from it. He died aged 74 at the County Hospital Portlaoise on Friday, 1st February after a short illness. His funeral took place at the local cemetery on Sunday with V. Rev. T Ryan, PP and Rev. G. O' Mahony, CC, reciting the prayers at the graveside. As member of a family with long associations with the town, 'The Gary' spent his entire lifetime there. He had his own philosophic way of looking at life. He loved to reminisce about 'the good old day's', and what was generally accepted as progress was seen by him in a different light. He had his own brand of wit and humour, and in his observations of people and events, he produced gems that will often be repeated.

Living next door to Tom Warren and Gary Doyle, lived Kit Lalor whose aunt had lived in the house before her. Next to Kit was Ned and Mary Delaney who always kept a few ducks at the back of the house. Philly Cass and his brother Jimmy lived in the next house. Philly could remember every score in an All-Ireland Final and who scored. He was an amazing man. Jimmy 'Scrapper' Lalor and his father lived next to them. Both operated a small business on the street at Ryan's corner in the town. When Maria was growing up, they sold fresh fish on a Friday.

The last two cottages were used for storage by the Council. Finally, the two large two-storey houses at the top of the street lived Mog Fitzpatrick and when he moved, Jimmy and Bernie Hartford moved in. Behind Jimmy's house, in the late 1890s and into the early 1900s, a Blacksmiths forge was built. The house was occupied by William Carty, a Blacksmith, and his nephew Thomas O' Flaherty, an apprentice to blacksmith. In 1984 and 1985, a total of 15 grenades were found buried in the garden presumed for the war effort that took place back in 1919. The forge itself has long been demolished. The very last house was occupied by Martin Cummins, he was

KNOCKNAMOE HOUSE

the last of eleven family members to live in this house. Toilets for the residents of Temperance Street, both men and women, were provided at the top of the street. This was effectively a shed built over a stream that was running underneath. Darcy Carthy a man that lived on the Ballinakill road and who was employed by the de Vesci Estate looked after the toilets for the tenants in my time living there.

Two toilet bowls with wooden seats, one for the men and one for the women, like a commode, were set directly over the stream. There were no doors or any type of privacy for the toilets. The stream that flowed underneath the toilet frames was the same one that flowed down along the boundary ditch between Casserly's and the Hospital on the Ballinakill road. The stream continued along the boundary between Delahanty's and where the old Workhouse was situated in the Council yard. It continued along the top end of Temperance Street until it joined another one that flowed along the Main Street of the town. This stream crossed the main road at the lower end of the town and eventually made its way down to the river Nore. This stream flowed freely down along the main street, I believe, until the 1940s before it was eventually covered over for health and safety reasons.

Decision made to level these Houses

The first of these little houses to be demolished were the ones directly behind Knocknamoe house in 1972. The maisonettes were built on that side of Temperance Street first, before knocking down the others on the opposite side in 1973 and 1974.

Call to Restore Little Houses

A call for restoration of the little houses in Temperance Street Abbeyleix was made by the Tidy Towns adjudicators in their 1973 report in the town. They saw the group of 130 years old dwellings as a conservation area of great potential and an area which is unique to Abbeyleix. They recommended the local Development Committee in associations with Laois Planning Authority to initiate a renewal scheme for the houses. It was something they suggested, that might be considered as a suitable project to undertake as a contribution to European Architectural Heritage Year in 1975. In addition, they pointed out that it would help to increase the stock of housing within the town itself and cut down the need for urban sprawl. Built in 1842 as a widows' rooms by a Protestant Temperance Society that was in existence in Abbeyleix at that time, the two rows of apartment dwellings became the property of the Laois County Council in recent years and the Council has planned to replace them with maisonettes. Long regarded as very sub-standard homes, a number of families were rehoused out of the Temperance Street houses some years ago and at present are occupied, for the most part, by unmarried people.

Abbeyleix Fire Brigade

In the early days of our newly formed State, the success rate of extinguishing a fire in Ireland was poor due to inadequate equipment that they were using. The lack of manpower and the supply of water contributed to the low success rate. Thankfully, the Fire Service has come a long way since they were first introduced into our towns and cities. Modern day equipment and a better supply of our natural water resources means that the success rate of extinguishing a fire has much improved. The Irish Free State, or 'Saorstát Eireann', was the name of Ireland from 1922 to 1937. It replaced the names of both the Irish Republic and Southern Ireland. The Government, called the Executive Council at the time, was headed by the President of the Executive Council, instead of a Prime Minister. The Government of Ireland was established on the 29th of December 1937. The State and the individual local authorities had a lot of work to do in order to improve the fire service and bring it up to the professional standard that we see today.

A Tragic Event
When I was growing up, the older generation of Abbeyleix often spoke about a tragic event that happened close to the town in September 1915. It was described as a House Inferno at the

time where a house close to Abbeyleix town was burned to the ground, and unfortunately a woman lost her life when she was burned to death. An article about the fire appeared in the newspaper the following week, describing it as 'an absolute tragic accident.' The fire started in the early hours on the 11th of September 1915 and set off a series of events which ultimately ended in failure due to a lack of firefighting capabilities. A Grandmother first noticed the fire in her house in the early hours of the morning. She first called her daughter, who in turn summoned the help of her young nephew and his friend who had been staying the night. The boys got on their bicycles and cycled into Abbeyleix looking for help. When the neighbours and people from the town arrived at the house to extinguish the fire, all they had was buckets and a shallow supply of water. Although the people did their absolute best to help, they soon found that they were completely out of their depth, resulting in the house being burned to the ground and the death of a woman that was still in the house.

How the Fire Service Began

Up until 1939, there was no formal fire brigade service in county Laois. Several volunteer firefighting units existed within the county. These volunteers were based in each of the larger towns spread throughout the county who were made up of unpaid people that were not accountable to anyone, they just served the local community.

In 1939, World War Two began and the Air Raid Precautions Act 1939 required local authorities to establish fire brigades to extinguish fires in towns with a population of 4,000 people and over. The only town in Laois to have a fire brigade was Portlaoise. The Fire Brigade Act 1940 further increased and strengthened the fire brigades and remained the primary fire service legislation until it was replaced by the Fire Service Act 1981. Portlaoise had been equipped with a trailer pump and other equipment. The trailer was located on lower main street in the town close to where Shaw's shop was located.

The only method of towing the trailer pump was by hackney car and several of the cars in the town were fitted with a tow bar to pull the trailer pump. However, if the car was unavailable the crew had to either wait for the car or push the trailer themselves. Other units were established throughout the county in locations where the volunteers existed. These units were equipped with hand carts manufactured by the Russell Brothers of Portarlington. The carts carried five lengths of canvas hose, a ladder, two buckets, a standpipe, key, and bar. These early units were known locally as 'ladder and bucket brigades' and were pushed by the firemen to the fire.

Abbeyleix began to operate their fire service similar to Portlaoise in early January 1950. If a fire was reported to them that was outside of the town limits, Jackie Bergin would be summoned. Jackie operated a hackney service in the town. He drove a Ford consul Mark II Saloon (204e). Although there was no draw bar on the car, there was a fitting on the fire brigades trailer pump that connected to the rear bumper of the car and off they went. This is how they travelled to Heywood college on the 31st of January in 1950 when the school went on fire. This fire was reported as 'an inferno' and was witnessed by people from miles around. The people from Abbeyleix reported as having witnessed this inferno from the top of Mitchells Hill close to the town.

Abbeyleix fire brigade carried out their weekly training at the old picture house in New Row opposite the brigade's premises. It was called the picture house at the time and later became known as the Milo Cinema. The children from New Row would watch the fire men climb their ladders up on to the roof of the cinema carrying sacks with contents in them equal to the weight of a person. The children gathered to watch this free show every Monday evening. Sean Carroll formerly from New Row, now in his eighty's, remembers being entertained as a young boy, along with lots of other children that lived on the street at the time.

After World War II ended, surplus trailer pumps were purchased from Great Britain and saw the establishment of the fire brigade on a countrywide basis. In 1956 seven land-Rover fire engines were purchased for £1200 each. Each land-rover was fitted with a pump, a water tank and a first aid line. Each one carried several lengths of canvas hose and assorted branch pipes. As the years went by these vehicles were augmented with the purchase of what are now recognize as fire appliances. Mobilization of the crew was another problem in the early years as the Air Raid Siren was not yet in use. The crew were called out by someone informing a member of the fire crew that there was a fire. The fireman had to then get on his bicycle and cycle to the next fireman's house or his employment and so on. This was the reason it took over twenty minutes to arrive at the scene of a fire at the Courthouse in Portlaoise on the main street in 1945, a distance of only a few hundred yards.

Air raid Sirens were also purchased from Great Britain after the war. They were located in each of the larger towns in Laois that had a fire brigade service. These were Abbeyleix, Stradbally, Rathdowney, Mountrath, Durrow, Portarlington, Ballinakill, Mountmellick, and Portlaoise. This happened throughout Ireland and became the standard method of alerting fire men to a fire. Up until the 1970s, the siren going off in the town alerted the locals that the fire brigade was needed as well as the firemen themselves. The first modern alerting system using pagers was introduced into county Laois in the 1960s. Portlaoise was the first town to avail of this system, however the rest of the county had to continue using the air raid siren for another few years.

Abbeyleix Brigade

Abbeyleix fire brigade moved into its first new premises in New Row when it was first officially offered to them in 1944. The premises was a disused dwelling house at the time that had been owned by a gifted saddler named Charlie Ring. Charlie moved from this address and settled down at another premises on the Portlaoise road where he lived out the rest of his life. Charlie lined collars, mended saddles, and stitched breeching to the timeless argument of journey-man card player. Journeyman, or journeyman's licence, is a certification granted to tradesmen upon completion of an apprenticeship. A tradesman who received this certification is referred to as a journeyman, of which Charlie certainly was one.

Jim Maher lived on the Ballyroan road and was the first District Officer to take charge. Jim was assisted by Sub-Officer Arthur Taylor, the Courthouse, First Leading Fireman,

Hugh O Connor, the Tiles, Second Leading Fireman Joe Mc Grath, Rathmoyle, Ordinary Firemen, James Quinn, the Tiles, Paddy Hill, the Ballinakill Road, Maurice Kelly, the Tiles, and William Bergin, a Blacksmith from New Row, uncle of the two famous GAA hurlers in the town at the time, the Bergin Brothers. In 1947, the first Air Raid Siren was erected on top of the office wall at the front of Bramley's Garage on the main street. This was activated by means of a break-glass-system erected on the front wall close to the entrance door of Bramley's office. This siren remained in place until it was removed and re-erected on the roof of the Town Hall in 1967.

In 1955, there was great excitement within the brigade when the men from Abbeyleix took possession of one of the seven Land-Rover fire engines that were purchased in Great Britain. This was certainly seen as a big improvement in their ability to extinguished fires compared to the equipment that they had to use up to that point. The Abbeyleix Land-Rover CI7904 was housed in their premises in New Row.

New Technology on the Way
Alerting fire men in the town when a fire was in progress still required someone to get on their bicycle and cycle to Bramley's Garage on the main street in the town to sound the alarm, and then remain there until a fire man came on the scene. When the firemen would arrive, they would ask where the fire was and go to it. This was the way it was always done. In 1956, new technology was on the way. Joe Mc Grath from Rathmoyle was the Sub Officer in the station at the time. He was chosen by the Chief Fire Officer from Portlaoise to have a telephone installed in his house for the fire brigade. In the event of a fire, people could ring and alert someone in the house that there was a fire.

Growing up, I lived on the same road as Joe Mc Grath. I'm sure it wasn't officially allowed but when our neighbours family members rang home from England and so on, they would ask to speak to one of their relatives that lived on the road. Someone from Joe's house ran to the neighbour's house and let them know that there was a phone call for them. I would see someone occasionally running down the road to Joe's house to take the call and witness the panicking as a consequence! It was not because the person that was on the other end of the phone was ringing from a telephone Kiosk, or otherwise known as a one-armed bandit at the time. The panic came from not knowing if somebody else may be trying to ring and report a fire at the same time.

New Fire Officers

Lots of changes occurred in Abbeyleix Fire station during 1975. Station Officer Joe Mc Grath decided to call it a day and retired from the service. Christy Phelan replaced him as Station Officer while Tim Bonham was appointed Sub Officer. These changes meant that the squad had been reduced to seven fire men. During the same year the squad returned to a full complement when Joe Mills from Thornberry joined the team.

Fireman Retires

1980 saw the break of the one remaining personal link Abbeyleix Fire Brigade had with the town's initial Brigade. Mr Paddy Hill, who had joined the brigade when it formed in 1944, retired from the service. He diligently served under four successive Station Officers.

Fire men call for new Premises

The Abbeyleix Firemen soon found that the premises that they were in since 1944 wasn't suitable for their needs at all. The entrance door into the building was only seven feet wide, which meant that the Land-Rover and fire tender only had an inch or two to spare when they tried to park it in the station. There was only sufficient space to allow the jeep and fire tender to reverse but all occupants, except the driver, had to exit the vehicle before reversing into the station. The entrance to the station had become dilapidated with the timber door decaying. Internal facilities were non-existent. Through the years the premises was allowed to deteriorate to hovel status. If you could visualise weeping walls, a leaking roof, draughty doors, no water or sewerage facilities, and a broken down 1800s open fireplace for heating, well then you are halfway there! Despite all its problems, Abbeyleix Fire Brigade had won more county titles than any other brigade in Laois. In 1985, the good news came after years of campaigning by local Councillor Jimmy Phelan and others for a more suitable premises to house the Fire Service, a decision was made to rehouse the Brigade in the town's Market House.

Old Soldier Dies

Widespread regret was caused in Abbeyleix by the death of Mr James Maher, from Ballyroan Road, at a Dublin hospital on Wednesday, 17th June 1973. He had been in failing health for some time and was in his late eighties. James was a member of a deeply rooted Abbeyleix family, and like so many young men of twenty, joined the British Army in the early 1900s. He served during World War I from 1914-1918 for which he was decorated. In later life, he gave his energy to local affairs and was the first Station Officer of the infant Abbeyleix Fire Brigade when it was first set up in 1944. Jim was always a staunch Labour supporter; he was a pillar of the local branch for many years. He was also secretary of the old age pension committee and was a valued member of the old Abbeyleix football club. When he died, he was survived by his son, daughters, sisters, and other relatives. He was interred in the Abbeyleix cemetery.

Christy Calls Time on his Career

Christy Phelan was a stalwart in the community and a proud Abbeyleix man all his life. He joined the Fire Service in 1950 and served the people of our town in an exemplary fashion. He also corresponded for the Leinster Express for over 40 years, Christy kept the whole community well informed about almost everything that was going on. He spent 38 years as a member of the fire service. He took over the role as Station Officer from Joe Mc Grath when Joe retired in 1975. Unfortunately, Christy never got to experience the long-awaited move to the new Station that had been promised since 1985. He missed out by only one year. The New Station opened in 1989 one year after Christy had retired from the service. Christy was always very highly thought of by the people of our town and beyond. Christy's 25th anniversary of his passing was in June 2021. Ar dheist Dé go raibh a h'anam dilis.

New Station Officer

Peter O Shea took over the helm in the Fire Station in 1988 replacing Christy. Peter remained in charge until 1990 until he retired from the service. He gave loyal service to the Fire Service throughout his career and only managed to enjoy 6 years in retirement when he unfortunately passed away in 2006. When Peter O Shea retired as Station Officer in 1990, Joseph 'Sonny' Tyrell replaced him. Tyrell remained in that position until 2014. He enjoyed the new Fire Service facilities when they had moved to the new location in the Market House in the previous year. He also oversaw the next location change when the Market House was deemed inadequate to cater for the modern professional Fire Service that we have today. The Fire Service had to move to the Macra Hall temporarily for a period of two years while the Market House was undergoing renovation work. The building was renovated into a modern library and Art Gallery, it was re-opened by way of town improvements.

During the renovation work in 2007, the World War Two Air Raid Siren was taken down from the building and incidentally is currently looking for a new home where it can be displayed along with the history related to this particular one. My preference would be, to have this Air Raid Siren erected and placed on show somewhere in this Heritage Town where it would certainly create a conversation piece for future generations. After all, it is part of our heritage now and may be of benefit where it would create an interesting subject for future generations to discuss in times to come. This siren served the community well for the 60 plus years that it was in existence here. The new Fire Station is now located on the Portlaoise Road close to the town. It officially opened on the 22nd of April 2008 by Mr Tony Killeen T D Minister of State for Environment and Energy. Mr Tom Lalor from Tea Lane is now the Station Officer, promoted in September 2014 while PJ Peacock from Rathmoyle took up the role of Sub Officer in the same year. Other members of the Abbeyleix Fire Service are, Anthony Coffey from Rathmoyle, Brian Keegan from Raheen,

Catherine Mansfield from Ballinakill, Timothy Bonham from Ballyroan, and Bosco Lalor from Ballytarsna.

Laois County Fire & Rescue Service
2022 has certainly seen huge advances in the fire and rescue service in the County since the beginning of the Irish State. There are now eight fire stations based in Laois, complete with a fully trained professional staff always ready for duty whenever they are called upon. The Abbeyleix Fire Brigade staff were thanked by the family of a man who was rescued from a serious accident that occurred on Main Street of the town. This man was trapped underneath an articulated lorry due to an accident in early January 2020. He was eventually rescued, and air lifted to Hospital. His family believe that his life was saved by the emergency services. This was only one of many feats, that our local fire and rescue service had been involved in throughout their long service in our town. Congratulations and well done to all the officers and fire men in Abbeyleix, for their dedication, hard work and for the service that they provide to all the families in our community.

Abbeyleix Fire Brigade 1960
Nine Fire Brigade Officers seen in the 1960 photograph is the oldest photograph in their possession, taken outside their first Fire Station in New Row.
Back Row (L/R): Hugh O Connor, Paddy Hill, Martin Dunne, Billy Whelan, Paddy Mc Hugh, Joe Mc Grath.

Front Row (L/R): John Gorman, Christy Phelan, Timmy Bonham.

Jimmy Hartford

Tribute to a Wonderful Abbeyleix Man

The people of Abbeyleix and indeed everyone that knew him will be saddened to learn that on the 25th of November 2022, it will be the 25th anniversary of James 'Jimmy' Hartford's passing. While on his way home after playing a gig in Eamonn An Chnoic's lounge in Raheen, Co. Laois, he was only 56 years of age when he passed away. Jimmy could certainly have been regarded as having been a legend in his own lifetime and loved by all who knew him.

Jimmy was a great family man in the first instance. He was married to Bernie Higgins in August 1968, Bernie was from Coolraine in Co Laois. Jimmy, Bernie, and their three sons Fergal, Bernard and Ronan lived in a house that they purchased in Temperance Street in the town. In 1995, they sold their home and purchased a new one in Abbey Crescent on the Ballyroan road. His son Bernard purchased the family home from his parents. He decided to rent the house and emigrated to Australia to see another part of the world.

Unfortunately, Jimmy only managed to enjoy his new home for two years before he passed away. I'm sure that everyone that knew Jimmy Hartford felt the same as I did when I heard of his passing. It came as an absolute shock. Jimmy's death has left a void in this community that has never been filled since. I feel privileged to have had Jimmy among one of my good friends. Jimmy led by example and sincerity. His enthusiasm was infectious, his personality was such that he never had a problem making friends no matter where he went. He loved his home and his community with a passion. The wheel has turned full circle now that his son Bernard has taken up a position in management in the last couple of years working in the same area where Jimmy was born and reared.

I first became friends with Jimmy Hartford back in 1968, when I signed up and became one of twenty-five other employees that worked in the Abbeyleix sawmills. Joe O' Brien from Abbeyleix managed the sawmills at the time. Jimmy was probably the most important cog in the wheel assisted by Pat

Mc Hugh from Rathmoyle. Jimmy's job description was described as a 'saw-doctor', a position he had taken over from Paddy Ring. Jimmy had the responsibility of keeping the blades of the industrial sized band saws always sharpened and ready for use.

Musical Genius

Jimmy Hartford became much more widely known as a musical genius. Back then we all probably took Jimmy's musical ability for granted, not realizing just how exceptionally talented he really was. Jimmy lived in Baggot's Park in Abbeyleix with his parents, brother John and three sisters. When he was only just a young boy attending school, Jimmy received a small accordion from his parents. His parents had already arranged for Jimmy to be tutored by Jackie Bergin from New Row. Jackie, a talented musician himself, had formed his own band in the town and entertained local people and people from the surrounding areas of Abbeyleix when they attended the Town Hall for dances, and so on.

Eddie O' Keeffe, from lower Boley Shanahoe, one of Jimmy's lifelong friends since the early 1950s. Eddie recalls that Jackie Bergin had little work to do teaching Jimmy how to play the accordion and indeed the harmonica as well. Jimmy's natural talent allowed him to become a competent accordion player in a short space of time. Jimmy and Eddie took up employment in the sawmills in 1955 when they were only 14 years of age. Eddie remembers Jimmy playing minor hurling for the Abbeyleix team. He hurled for the sawmill team as well. There was great excitement among the sawmill staff when Jimmy was invited to play his accordion on the Ceilí House show presented by Seán O'Murchú who was the presenter of the radio show at the time. This show went on air every Saturday night at ten o clock pm. All the great bands played on this show over the years, such as the Tulla, Kilfenora, Mayglass, Mc Cusker Bros, Johnny Pickering, and the Gallowglass Céilí band.

The weekly listenership for Céilí House exceeded one million people. At a time of high emigration from Ireland, there are accounts of Irish workers in London climbing lamp posts on Saturday nights, radio in hand in the hope of getting a better reception for their weekly link with music and song they had left at home in Ireland. All the Abbeyleix sawmill staff tuned in to the show to listen to Jimmy play his accordion on the Saturday night Céilí House show early in 1968. He had produced a stunning performance on the night and was congratulated by everyone when he arrived in for work on the following Monday morning. Jimmy felt that this was no big deal, he just took it all in his stride.

Jimmy had a long association with Céilí House during the 1960s. One of the shows that he took part in was uploaded by *mrCeilman* onto *YouTube* on the 6th of January 2013. It was lovely to listen back and hear Jimmy doing what he did best, just listening to the beautiful sound of Traditional Irish Music performed by the one and only. Jimmy played two hornpipes and two Reels on the show. The sawmill Christmas party that was held each year, from 1968 right up to 1972 before I left and tried to make my way in the world, were great fun. The parties usually consisted of a dinner dance and the musical entertainment provided by Jimmy and his good friend Pat Tynan from Killamuck, Abbeyleix.

Reminiscing with some of the sawmill staff members some years later, we decided unanimously that those days were by far the greatest days of our lives, otherwise known as the 'Good Old Days.'

The Vic Loving Company

The Vic Loving Company produced brilliant shows. They travelled from one town to another throughout the country performing top class variety and local talent competitions back in the late 1940s, 1950s, and into the 1960s as well. Lal Deegan wrote in an article in 1983 that the Vic Loving Company performed much better variety shows back then compared to the rubbish you would see on television now! The company also promoted local talent competitions which provided an opportunity for the local artists to show the public just what they could do on stage. These shows were held in the Town Hall in Abbeyleix with a full crowd.

Eddie, Jimmy, and few other friends decided to encourage Jimmy to enter one such talent competition that was being held in the Town Hall on a Sunday night during the winter of 1955. Jimmy was only around 14 years of age at the time. The Town Hall was packed to the rafters on the night when Jimmy took to the stage. He wore a tweed suit with short trousers. He had a new mother-of-pearl button accordion that he had just purchased after saving up his money for a long time. This accordion could produce a fantastic sound as long as it was in the right hands. Jimmy played a couple of tunes in the competition.

The very first tune Jimmy Hartford ever played in public was at this event, which was 'Zambezi' by Lou Busch. When he finished playing the tune, he received a standing ovation. The audience brought the house down so to speak with continuous applause. The adjudication for the competition was by way of the audience response to the act after it had been performed. Needless to say, Jimmy won the competition hands down, and was now well on his way to becoming the brilliant musician that he eventually became. Jimmy was a naturally gifted musician, even though he could not read music. He was drawn to the accordion like a magnet when he was a young boy and he only needed to hear a tune once before he too could play the same tune.

The Milo Cinema

The Courtney Brother's arrived at Abbeyleix town where they put on a variety show for the public in the Milo cinema. This venue was used after it had already ceased showing films earlier in 1971. The Courtney's were originally a Circus outfit that came to town on an annual basis for a short number of years where they entertained the public. They followed the more famous circus at the time called Duffy's Circus. The Circus was always held in Dan Cass's field in Balladine where the people from the town and surrounding areas as well would come in their hundreds to attend.

The Courtney's invited the public to enter a talent competition that they were holding in conjunction with their own variety show in the Milo cinema. On this occasion, some of the sawmill staff pleaded with Jimmy to enter the competition. On the Sunday night in January 1972, the sawmill staff arrived to see the show. The old cinema was full on the night. When Jimmy sang and performed his tunes on the accordion, all his supporters of which they were many went wild with applause resulting in Jimmy becoming the most popular act on show. Jimmy claimed first place in the competition on the night, much to the delight of his followers.

Set Dancers

Jimmy had a great love of Irish traditional music as well, he had embraced with determination the native music, song, and dance of the Irish people. He teamed up with Maura Shanahan for several years providing the music for her Irish dancers when they performed Hornpipes, Jigs and Reels, locally and nationally.

Camross Cashel Set Dancers

The Camross Cashel Set Dancers, not only known throughout the county but the country as well. They headed off to Luton, England to represent Ireland in a dancing competition in 1977. Photo on this post show the dancers just before they set off to take part in the competition. Front Row: Paddy Carey, Lourda Carey, Jimmy Hartford (musician), Mary Conroy, Paddy

Doheny. Back Row: Stephen Conroy, Marie Higgins, John Lupton, Annette Dunne, and Martin Delaney.

Coolraine Men off to sing in America

A competition that was run by Aer Lingus in March 1979, 'Search for Stars', allowed the winners to sing in America. Described in a newspaper article at the time, as taking place, "in the well papered backroom, with the crowd listening quietly and tape recorder hidden behind the curtains, the Coolraine Quartet were playing. Down the road, in Sheeran's pub where it all began, the backdrop of wooden barrels and open fireplaces was different but the sound of "The Silver Spoon" rendered by the lads was as hearty as ever. Jimmy Hartford, playing accordion, Tim Bergin on fiddle, Joe 'Banjo' Burke, and Sean White on the flute, are the members of the Coolraine Quartet which won the competition. The prize was two weeks of 'Sessionising', and seeing the sights, playing where and when they want. Aer Lingus had arranged five engagements for their first week, including a booking on St, Patrick's night and after that the band said they would play it by ear."

Stressing that they entered the competition in the first place for the 'craic', the band said that while they had enjoyed the last few months with engagements in pubs around the county, their music remains strictly for pleasure only. Although the four members of the band are in the timber business, their initial formation resulted from informal sessions in Sheerans pub in Coolraine. Tim Bergin, who is vice-chairman of Camross Comhaltas, and Jimmy Hartford had been playing for about eight years in the pub. Sean White joined them and competed in the Scór competition getting as far as the Leinster final before they were knocked out. In the final line up, Joe Burke played with them.

Qualified in five Rounds

To get to the finals of the 'Search for Stars' competition the group had to qualify in five rounds. They found that as the competition progressed, it became much stiffer. They felt that it was really at the Leinster final stage that their own sound satisfied them, and they still would have liked to have had more time to rehearse new selections and re-arrange their songs. The most enjoyable venues for the Coolraine Quartet were the small pubs where the audience had a genuine appreciation of traditional music. Since the band's own musical preferences were hornpipes, Jigs, reels and the old songs. Once they were in America the Coolraine Quartet realised that they would have to concede somewhat to an Irish American audience, but they were looking forward to the prospect.

Afterwards, "we'll revert to our former obscurity," said Sean White with Joe Burke joking, "tell them to bury us at sea if anything happens to the plane."

Geraldine O' Keeffe

Geraldine O' Keeffe remembers Jimmy well. When she was a young girl, she remembers Jimmy coming to play his music in her parents' home accompanied by Tony Kennedy, her brother who also played the accordion. They would sing, dance and play music long into the night. Pat Tynan and Oliver Kenna from Knapton Abbeyleix were brilliant musicians and singers providing great entertainment for the large crowds of people that would attend these sessions in Geraldine's home. Her parents' home was regarded as somewhat of a Rambling house back in those days. Her sister Rose eventually did a line with Jimmy's brother John, who was also a very talented man in his own right. He was a brilliant man to whistle a tune and if he did Jimmy would pick up on it immediately. John and Rose eventually married and moved away to Ferbane in County Offaly to live. John passed away a young man at the age of 54. When Geraldine grew up, she met her husband Eddie O' Keeffe from Abbeyleix. They became accomplished Irish set dancers, as a result of their long association with Jimmy Hartford. One of Geraldine and Eddie's first public appearances performing a set dance was on the Late Late Show with presenter Gay Byrne on Saturday night the 21st March1987. This was where their set dancing career began.

Hawthorn Set Dancers

The Hawthorn public house in Ballacolla had a formidable dancing outfit that represented the Pub in set dancing competitions throughout Leinster. They danced to a high standard, 100% better according to Geraldine especially when Jimmy Hartford played the music. The Hawthorn lady set dancers had quite a few stars on the team to name but a few; Geraldine O' Keeffe, Grace Bergin, Josephine Byrne, Annette Duff, Marie Higgins, Anita Bonham, Mary Hearns, Mary O Keeffe, and Eileen Phelan. In whatever venue Jimmy played in, if he knew that Geraldine O' Keeffe was there he would always play her three favourite pieces of music. These were the *Sally Gardens, O' Sullivan's John,* and *Harvest Home/Ms Nc Clouds Reel*. He would often play and sing another one or two of his own favourite songs while performing at a venue like Gentle Annie, Harvest Moon. His favourite one of all was the *Lights of Rosslare Harbour* by P. J. Murrihy. A few of the bands that Jimmy was associated with over his lifetime entertaining the masses were the Statesmen, the Regency Trio, and the Country Ramblers. The Hawthorn set dancers were saddened beyond words, as was everyone that knew Jimmy, when Jimmy passed away. His passing saddened the set dancers so much that they didn't have the will to carry on dancing after Jimmy passed away, effectively ending the Hawthorn set dancers performing in public again. The void that was created with his passing has never been filled, and I believe that it can never be.

An Appreciation

Tobins favourite, the Harvest Home, The Boys of Bluehill and the liveliest polkas imaginable - these were the tunes played by the most gifted, talented accordionist to ever accompany a set dancing group. When Camross Set dancers took to the stage during their competition years, there were nine of them. Sitting behind the microphone was the reason they enjoyed so much success. Jimmy as one adjudicator so eloquently put it - "you knew the music was built into their shoes." Such was the affinity between him and the dancers.

Sean Carroll

Sean Carroll from Sweet-view Abbeyleix, another good friend of Jimmy Hartford, worked in the sawmill when Jimmy and Eddie O Keeffe arrived there to work in 1955. Not only did they become work colleagues, but they became good friends. They became great supporters and loved Jimmy's music like so many other people, and their friendship stood the test of time and lasting throughout the years. Sean recalls that it was a miracle Jimmy was ever able to play music again after an accident that he had in the sawmills in the early 1960s. Jimmy stood beside an industrial size wood planer one morning while chatting to

Patsy Watchorn and Jimmy Hartford.

Sean. As they talked, Jimmy began to rub his hand up and down over the cold steel blade on the planer which had been switched off at the time. Another employee arrived over to the machine with a piece of timber that he needed planed. Without noticing that Jimmy and Sean were chatting right beside the planer, the machine turned on, the motor roared into operation emitting a deafening sound, and Jimmy hit the floor screaming in agony. The tops of his fingers on one hand had been cut off. Sean Carroll immediately grabbed an old towel that was close by and wrapped it tightly around Jimmy's hand. Arrangements were quickly made to rush Jimmy to Portlaoise Hospital for medical treatment. An anxious wait at the Hospital for news on Jimmy's condition brought good news. It took Jimmy a long time to recuperate after this accident, but eventually did so and began to play the accordion again almost better than he had done before. This was truly a miracle.

Dynamite
While these men worked in the sawmills, health and safety hadn't been invented yet. Health & Safety was only introduced in 1989, replaced in 2005 by Safety Health and Welfare at work act. One of the jobs that Sean had to perform was when a big tree was brought into the mill to be cut, and if it was deemed too large for the saw, he would use dynamite to split it. Basically, a hole would be drilled into the butt end of the tree using an augur, which was a spiral-shaped tool. When the hole was drilled the dynamite was pushed into the hole, filled with sawdust and a fuse attached. Sean would light the fuse and run away as fast as he could before the dynamite would explode. The explosion would blow the tree in half making it possible then to saw the tree in the mill. There was an old shed at the back of the mill where the dynamite was stored with an old faulty lock used to secure it.

Sean remembers hearing that Leo Mills from the Portlaoise road went into the dynamite shed one day and took a piece of the dynamite home with him just to see what it was like. He sat close to the fire along with his brother Pat who began waving a small piece of it in front of the fire. It suddenly caught fire and exploded in his hand blowing off all the fingers on one of his hands. The policy of storing the dynamite in a shed at the back of the mill changed quickly after that!

The Piper

Jimmy loved to sing an old traditional song named the Piper, not so much at the dance venues but rather at an impromptu music gathering, or in a pub session. People loved to listen to the words of this old song, some of his friends would request it at every opportunity, and often join in and give their own version of it. The words of the song go like this:

Mrs Gilhooley gave a good party one night
She invited us all to attend,
We gathered a gang, jumped down to her house
A few pleasant hours for to spend.

There was Duffy and Charlie and Flynn and meself
Well, a crowd wasn't hard for ta find,
But the t'ing most important we almost forgot
We near' left the piper behind

We invited him down to the party
He brought his bagpipe just by chance
We asked him to sing, but he says, "AH, no"
But offered us a bit of a dance.

He picked up his pipes, he started to play
Someone got foolin' about
And cut a great hole in the bag of his pipes
And here is the tune that came out:

Naaaa, needeleedelum needeligh needeleedeleedel
num nee nigh daloh dalah daleedeleedel
lumdeeligh daligh daloh dadeedeleedel
dalumdeeligh dalohdaleedeleedeligh

When the piper found out that his bag, it was cut
Sure, he gave a great leap on the floor
And he slipped about in a quick hammer style
And he landed him under the jaw.

Mrs, Levi, she fainted, they all made a rush

Trying to get out of the door
But the piper had nine of them takin' the count
And he swore he would lick twenty more.

Well, if ever ya go to a party
Ah, you'd better keep this in your mind
Don't get vexed with the piper
For you'll find him a gentleman kind.

But if trouble should start keep out of his way
For he carries an awful punthone
Ah, you won't hear it comin' but whoop when it lands
Sure, you'll know it's an Irish chiteaugh.

Jimmy makes the front Page

On the 26th of April 1985, Jimmy was digging in the garden at the back of his house, assisted by his young son Ronan when he got the biggest surprise of his life. He found explosives in the garden. In the newspaper read, it went on to say that, "A man who was digging in his garden at the weekend made an unusual find - a mini arsenal. Mr Jimmy Hartford of Temperance Street, Abbeyleix, dug up eight hand grenades in the plot at the back of his home. Mr Hartford was accompanied by his young son Ronan. He alerted local Gardai, an Army explosives unit was immediately called.

"Shortly afterwards a controlled explosion was carried out by army experts from the Explosive Ordnance Demolition Unit from the Curragh Camp. Last year seven grenades were found in the same area and again the army was called in. The army unit confirmed that the grenades were dps (drill purpose) and that the area is now safe. A thorough inspection was carried out with the aid of metal detectors. It is believed that the grenades may have been buried during the troubled times."

Jimmy would not have known that there was a foundry built at the back of his house in the late 1890s and recorded again in 1911. A man by the name of William Carty a Blacksmith and Thomas O' Flaherty an Apprentice to Blacksmith work was a nephew of his as well as a lodger named John Phelan an agricultural labourer lived at that address. This was eight years before the War of Independence which began on the 21st of January 1919 and lasted until the 11th of July 1921. Making grenades in Abbeyleix wasn't unusual at that time. The Mc Hugh Family also made them for the war effort at their foundry in New Row in the town. The grenade casings when made by the blacksmiths in the foundry were then buried in the ground and hidden in various other places because the Black and Tans knew the grenades were being made in the Blacksmiths Forges in the town and despite searching their premises, they never managed to find any.

Jimmy Hartford-A Memory

The music in your fingers always enthralled me
They ran up and down the keyboard with grace and charm
Bringing life and joy to eager ears
Your fingers, your voice bade me farewell
And welcomed me home again
We often played together and laughed together with
uncontrollable glee
When finger slipped and melodies were re-arranged
The slips were mine the perfection yours
My goings away, my returns, were
Entwined in your athletically fingers and melodious voice
How I loved it!
Today we played together
In my mind's eye and remembered the past
Today you were called to finger a different instrument
Maybe a harp, perhaps your beloved accordion
I cannot visualise you without that beloved instrument
Strapped around your shoulders and your voice rendering
Melodies of happiness, joy and sadness
Today your voice is still, yet you speak to me, like your brother
John
"I've only slipped away into the next room
Call me Jimmy, laugh as we've always laughed
Play as we've always played Life means all that it ever meant"
Your music lives on, from Eamonn 'n Chnoic to Cairo,
From Cape Town through to Karoo, to high-rise Johannesburg
You continue to bring happiness across the globe

Farewell Jimmy, Hello Jimmy.

Written by Ben Kennedy (Lower Boley and South Africa)

Every name mentioned in this post, all his family, friends and indeed everyone that knew Jimmy Hartford felt absolutely devastated when they heard of his passing. His likes will never be seen again. I'm sure everyone will agree that it has been an absolute pleasure to have known this man. We extend our sympathy's again to Bernie, Fergal, Bernard, and Ronan as his 25th anniversary of his passing comes ever closer. Ar dheis Dé go raibh a h'anam dilis - May his holy soul be on the right side of God.

Abbeyleix ICA

ICA 80th Birthday Party 1994.

An Emotional Goodbye
On the 13th of July 2022, a function was held in the Abbeyleix
Heritage House to celebrate the life and times, and indeed the
end of ICA in Abbeyleix. What a sad day for the last remaining
Lady members of Abbeyleix ICA. The Ladies never envisaged
that this day would come, or indeed that they would be around
to witness the end of this fabulous organisation. Memories were
rekindled, laughter and a few tears were shed when the time
came to finally say goodbye to ICA in Abbeyleix. Truly the end
of an era.

The Beginning
Abbeyleix ICA held its first meeting on a cold and wintry night
on the 26th of January 1914. The first recorded meeting was
held in the coffee shop known as the Coffee Palace situated in
the square in Abbeyleix town. The Guild was first registered on
the 14th of February 1914. Incidentally, this was the same
address that William Henry Gillispie gave when he purchased a
ticket for the Titanic in Patrick Ryan's shop on Main Street
Abbeyleix in 1912. 1914 is also remembered for another reason,
it was the beginning of the First World war. The purpose of the
first initial meeting was to set up and organise a milk depot and

sell it at the lowest price possible for the people who could not afford to purchase it in sufficient quantities for their families at the time. The thinking behind this was something similar to what Lady Emma De Vesci did some 69 years earlier when she set up soup kitchens in the town to feed the poor and destitute during the Famine years beginning in 1845. The affordable milk scheme that the Ladies set up at that time went on up until 1924 when by that time the local milk supplies had increased and therefore became more affordable for the families that availed of it.

Ladies with a Vision

The ladies from the town that spearheaded this wonderful organisation were made up of President Mrs T Fitzherbert, Ms Kemis, and Mrs I Fitzherbert. Their committee included Mrs Campbell, Lady Poe, Mrs H Orme, Ms Murphy, Mrs King, Mrs Barr, Mrs Smith. Viscount De Vesci, Fr Lalor, Admiral Sir Edward Poe, and H.I. Fitzherbert also played their part in the organisation. At the time, life for women in rural Ireland was one of hardship and drudgery and the ICA set out to offer friendship, hope, support, and leadership. Unfortunately, the minutes book from 1914 to 1935 went missing resulting in lots of valuable information being lost. Meetings were held subsequently in the Old Court House from 1934 after the Ladies had moved from the Palace coffee shop

1954

1954 brought an unforgettable Abbeyleix branch of the ICA. The women were given a house by Lady Susan De Vesci at Lower Main Street, and it became known from that point on as the ICA House. The Ladies decorated the house and made it as comfortable as possible. They also tended to the garden and spent many enjoyable years there until 1999 when the house returned to the De Vesci Family. The ICA Ladies held their meetings from that point on in the Social Services House in New Row in the Town.

Golden Jubilee 1964

The Macra Hall, or otherwise called the young farmers club at the time, was booked by the Ladies of the Abbeyleix ICA to celebrate their Golden Jubilee. The secretary, Mrs Evelyn Whelan, along with the committee organised the event which turned out to be a huge event at the time. Mrs Cannie Deniffe wrote a song especially for the occasion. Copies of the song were distributed to all the members where they were encouraged to learn the words so that they could perform it on the night. The President, Mrs Mary Moran, thanked the 126 people that attended the celebration dinner. They enjoyed the entertainment provided for them which included the Irish dancers that won the regional finals of the Eleanor Gibbon trophy. Representatives from the young farmers performed songs made famous by the Clancy brothers and music was supplied by the Everglades show band. Rita Mc Donnell and Mrs Evelyn Whelan gave solo singing performances as well.

A copper beech tree was planted in the front garden of the ICA House in June 1965 and continued to grow as did the hopes and dreams of the Abbeyleix members of the ICA. It is important to note that the new age of technology had not been conceived by this time and so all the Lady members played a key role in encouraging other young women to join and participate in a host of activities and skills which the Guild had fine-tuned over the years. It has always been said that every day is a school day, you learn something new every day. I believe all the Lady members would testify that they learned something new every day and became much more confident and assertive in communicating and expressing their thoughts, feelings, and opinions due to being members of the Abbeyleix ICA. The Ladies always remembered to celebrate milestones like their 50th, 75th, 80th, and 90th anniversaries of the ICA in Abbeyleix.

100-year celebration
2014 was the biggest and most important year of all. It was the 100th year anniversary of the Abbeyleix branch of the ICA. The Abbeyleix branch was the second oldest guild in the country, with Bree in county Wexford being the first founded in May 1910 by a small group of well-educated young women. Its aim was 'to improve the standard of life in rural Ireland through

Education and Co-operative effort.' The organization was non-denominational and non-party political, principles which has continued to this day.

13th of July 2022
July 2022 brought about a sad evening for the remaining Lady members of the Abbeyleix ICA as they recalled the date that they joined this wonderful organization where they made so many new friends and learned new skills that have benefited their lives. The world is a changed place since the Guild was formed over 108 years ago. The dwindling number of new Lady members in the ICA was due in no small way to the new age technology that we are all becoming so familiar with. If you have a smart phone and computer now, you have instant access to all your friends while using social media such as *Facebook*, *Twitter*, *Instagram*, *Snap-chat*, emails and all the rest. Tutorial videos on YouTube if you want to learn how to fix something or learn how to make or do basically anything. Coupled with all this new technology, it's easy to see how difficult it became for the Lady members of the ICA to attract younger women to join.

The Guild can be so proud of itself for what it has achieved over the years. The ICA Ladies were instrumental in organising and entering Abbeyleix Town into their first National Tidy Towns competition in 1959. As we are all very much aware of now just how important that decision was, particularly this year in 2022. I would like to wish a huge congratulations to all the Tidy Town volunteers, and indeed their committee. The people that somehow share willingly and generously their spare time, when huge numbers of them come out on a weekly basis and work hard to keep this beautiful town of Abbeyleix in such a lovely condition. The local Guild were key players in helping to organise the very successful Maytime festival established in 1970, they also added their weight when calling for the Towns first set of traffic lights to be installed.

An interesting story that's told about the time when the traffic lights were first installed in the Town in 1968. It was the fact that there was a local character named Chrissie 'Hopper' Delaney that lived on the Ballyroan Road at the time. Chrissie worked for Mr PJ Lalor who operated a thriving business on upper Main Street in the town. Chrissies looked after the household needs of the family at the time. They had welcomed a man from Tipperary who had taken up a new position of manager of the shop named Dan Murphy who himself became very well-known and liked by all throughout the local area.

Paddy Lalor found that his spare time had been completely taken up with politics at the time, and this influenced his decision to employ a manager to run the shop. The traffic lights were installed in the square, a local Garda named Tom Mc Grath stood on duty there. His job was to inform the local pedestrians on how to cross the road safely and correctly. Tom observed Chrissie walking down the street, she walked out across the main street to cross over to the shops. He shouted at her to return to where he was standing at the lights which she did.

"Now," Chrissie said, "Tom I just want to explain to you the proper way to cross the road here from the lights."

He said, "Do you see that button there? You press that and wait for the little green man to come on. When you see him, then it will be safe to cross the road."

Chrissie never stuck for an answer replied, "Will that little green man get Dan Murphy his dinner?" And off she stormed, leaving Tom to scratch his head in disbelief.

108 years of ICA in Abbeyleix

108 years has been a remarkable achievement to all the Ladies of the ICA in
Abbeyleix and for the role they played in keeping this wonderful organisation alive and well for as long as was humanly possible. It's not possible now to capture the108 years of history in just a few paragraphs. For people out there that would like to read more about the wonderful history of the ICA in Abbeyleix, the Guild published a book on their 100-year anniversary in 2014. I would like to take this opportunity the wish the remaining Lady members a long life and continued happiness in the future. To the Ladies now left with the unenviable job, which is to wind down and say goodbye, to 108 years of ICA in Abbeyleix. The President of the Spink branch of the ICA, Ms Anne Cass, officiated at this event spoke very

kindly about the Abbeyleix Guild and the lifelong friends she made over the years. And so, with a heavy heart it is time now to call time and wind up the Abbeyleix branch of the ICA for the last time.

Finally, a message to Catherine Smith, the last Lady to hold the position of secretary of the Abbeyleix Guild, that she may consider approaching the local branch of the library and ask them to safely store the minutes of all the meetings which they have in their possession. There is no doubt that some future generation will want to trawl through them some time in the future. God Bless You All.

Abbeyleix Hospital

The people from Abbeyleix and surrounding areas have felt proud that we have always had a hospital in our town during our lifetime. Things looked very different in November 2011 when at least 3,000 people turned out to protest because the HSE were threatening to close it. Bridget O' Neill, spokesperson for the patients in the hospital in which she was one herself, held up a sign at the protest which said she was a celebrity and that 'you can't get me out of my home.' Thankfully now in 2022, things look a lot brighter. Work is underway in a bid to complete an extension to the hospital and so the future is looking brighter. There is a great sense of achievement here, especially for the people that spearheaded the protest in 2011, when they realize that the HSE took on board the idea that they had submitted during the consultation process following the High Court ruling setting aside the decision to close the hospital in 2012. The hospital is now being used as a district health hub for South Laois.

In The Beginning
In the beginning, the hospital was built close to the site of the present day one. It was not a nice place to be in. The original building was located in what is now known as the Community Nursing Unit, which still exists today. In 1838, the Irish Poor

Law Act passed into law by the British House of Commons. Its purpose was to house the thousands of starving and destitute Irish people throughout the country.

The 2nd Viscount John de Vesci was a conscientious Landlord and had the best interest of the people of Abbeyleix foremost in his mind. He was one of only a small number of people who voted against the Poor Law Act in the House of Commons at the time. It was argued that the workhouses if built would become a 'Prison for the Poor', and that's exactly what happened.

The notorious workhouses in Ireland were built at this time and were run by a Board of Guardians who were themselves directed from Dublin. The workhouses and Hospitals throughout the Country were staffed by the sisters of Charity, St Vincent de Paul. The Board of Guardians ruled the Abbeyleix workhouse and the other workhouses in a very rigid and regimental way. There were three workhouses built in County Laois at this time. The first was Abbeyleix which opened in June 1842, the second was opened in January 1845 in Mountmellick, and the last one was opened in September 1853 in Donaghmore. The Abbeyleix workhouse was built with dark grey limestone, with narrow diamond shaped windows that were designed to allow a minimal amount of natural light in.

Abbeyleix Workhouse

Head of The Union

Abbeyleix was chosen as head of the Union covering an area from Timahoe to Durrow, and from Aghaboe to Ballinakill. The unions of Athy, Carlow and Roscrea also extended into the county. By 1849, fever hospitals in Mountrath and Doonane operated alongside twenty-one dispensaries in the county. Donaghmore Poor Law Union was dissolved in 1886. The contract for the building of the workhouse was signed in 1840 and was designed to accommodate 500 people. The cost of building the workhouse, which was on a 6-acre site at the time, was €6,900 and the work that had started in 1840 was finished in early June 1842. A mortuary was built at the south end of the workhouse and beyond that lay a burial ground. There is no evidence of this burial ground there today which is a great pity.

Famine in 1845

With the onset of the famine, the workhouse soon filled and overflowed with 'paupers.' When a fever broke out, conditions were horrendous. One wing was set aside in the workhouse for patients suffering with a fever, which had been brought about because of malnutrition and poverty. Run by a regime that separated families as soon as they entered, husbands and wives were separated from each other and their children. Many children were orphaned when their parents died from the rampant fever that had spread amongst the inmates. Several orphaned girls were put on boats and sent out to Australia.

　　Twenty-eight young Abbeyleix girls found themselves on boats heading to Australia in the years leading up to 1848. It may have seemed like a charitable policy to the authorities at the time and many of the young girls may have been much better off eventually. But it must have been a most distressing time both for the children and any relatives they were leaving behind, relatives who through no fault of their own and because of their own circumstances would not have been able to look after them. In the mid-1840s, two houses were rented to accommodate an additional 100 patients. Both houses were situated in Ralish. The first one is where Dick Kennedy now lives, and the other one belongs to the Kirwan family which is directly opposite. Both houses were co-joined in a large u-shaped courtyard.

Living in the Workhouse
The poor unfortunate people that lived in the workhouse had to work for their keep. The men broke stones that were then sold for the making of roads, building work, etc. They also worked on the farm, whitewashed the buildings, and looked after the gardens. The women scrubbed the wooden flooring in the workhouse. They were responsible for the laundry, kitchen, ironing, making their own clothes and much more. The reward for the men and women for the privilege of living there was their breakfast which consisted of seven ounces of oatmeal and a pint of buttermilk. Dinner consisted of three pounds of potatoes and one pint of buttermilk.

No Luxuries
No tea or tobacco was allowed. No meat was allowed or given to the paupers except on Easter Sunday and Christmas day. Some of the paupers that liked to smoke had to make do with white turf which was plentiful here in Abbeyleix. One pauper was reported to the Board of Guardians for chain smoking. It was suspected that he was stealing the tobacco. An enquiry was held. The interviewer asked the pauper about his excessive smoking and said, "I believe you are a very heavy smoker?"

"Indeed I am" the pauper replied. "Two bags of turf a week Sir."

1841 Census
The census of 1841 separated housing into four categories - the lower class being for the most part one room mud huts, built with organic material totally unfit for human habitation. 45% of rural housing in Ireland was in this category in 1841. While most inhabitants of the town of Abbeyleix occupied good quality stone-built houses with thatched roofs, as well as the tenants of Lord de Vesci they too were also adequately housed. There were however many in the area who were quite destitute. In many cases, these unfortunate souls chose the workhouse

where conditions, though quite abysmal, were preferred to those in which they would otherwise have had to live and where there was a least some food available. By the end of 1844, 466 people lived in the Workhouse built on what is now part of the County Council yard. The ambulance that was stationed there was a four-wheel horse drawn wagon, painted a dull red colour. The workhouse ambulance was driven by a pauper whose job it was to go and collect others from around the town and then take him or her back to the workhouse for a life of misery. The building that housed the workhouse horse drawn ambulance was later used to house the modern day one which had been driven by Gerry Higgins who lived in Rathmoyle Abbeyleix.

The de Vesci Family During the Famine Years

John, 2nd Viscount, de Vesci's eldest son, Thomas, was very active and influential in the Abbeyleix area as his father advanced in years during the time of the famine. The de Vesci family can never be accused of being absentee Landlords during those horrible years, or indeed at any other time during their time living in Abbeyleix. They created employment for lots of people living in the area. They also drastically reduced the rents or had forgiven them altogether during this time. Thomas de Vesci's wife, Lady Emma, set up soup kitchens in Abbeyleix and saved the lives of many hundreds of people for that there is no doubt. Thomas caught the famine fever during this time, but mercifully, recovered. His father John 2nd Viscount lived up until 1855. Thomas succeeded him and became the 3rd Viscount from that point on. It is interesting to note that the de Vesci family adopted an open policy. It was the only estate in the country that wasn't completely walled in and hidden from the public. The people from Abbeyleix have always held the de Vesci family in high regard. Doctor Boswell was the GP in Abbeyleix during the famine years. Regarded as an unsung hero at the time, his hard work and effort saved many lives of people that were in real need of medical assistance. He was held in very high esteem by all the people that lived in the area. Doctor Boswell lived at Woodville in Abbeyleix (now Casserly's). When he died, he was interred in the old Church graveyard within the Demesne.

An Investigation of the Records Began

A detailed study of the Workhouse records was excellently carried out by Martin Fennelly from Rathmoyle. Martin studied the records for a number of years prior to his passing on the 20th of December 1986. Martin paints a grim picture of life and conditions inside that institution at the time. When these unfortunate inmates died, they were transported by horse and cart to a corner of a field known as the 'Paupers' Graveyard', which is about half a mile from the Hospital

Martin Fennelly.

as you travel up along the Carlow Road and situated on the left-hand side down a narrow lane. The graveyard situated close to the workhouse was soon filled during the early famine years, causing a headache for the Board of Guardians as they needed to find another graveyard. They soon identified somewhere they could dispose of the bodies. This graveyard known locally as the 'Shank-Yard.' It was the burial ground for an estimated 2000 men, women, and children. At least one baby recorded as being just three days' old is buried here, named Michael. They were all from the local and surrounding areas of Abbeyleix, which included others that were not living in the workhouse but were nevertheless destitute. Most of these people died during the famine time as well as the poor unfortunates that had been inmates in the workhouse at the time.

The Passing of Time

Over 140 years passed before anything was done to indicate that this was a Christian burial ground. None of these people received any kind of prayer ceremony when they were buried here in mass graves at the time. No politicians or clergymen attended these burials. Martin Fennelly, and indeed his family, have to be commended for the interest and concern that they had for these poor unfortunate people. They set about highlighting and informing the public about the events that happened here in the place they called the 'Shank- Yard.' Martin received opposition from at least one person as he tried to reclaim this small piece of sacred ground and thank God he persisted. At least now we have somewhere to go and say a prayer for all the poor unfortunate souls that were buried here. This is our heritage whether it is a good news story or not.

Final Wishes

On Sunday the 11th of September 1994, Martin Fennelly's wishes were finally fulfilled when Fr Patrick Keogh Parish Priest of Abbeyleix assisted by Fr. Patrick Finnerty, celebrated Mass for the poor souls that were buried in this graveyard. Martin named it the 'Gateway to Heaven.' The Mass was attended by many local people, as well as Martin Fennelly's own family. Since then, the Fennelly family have taken it upon themselves to take care of this graveyard and is now always kept in a clean and tidy condition. I hope that in the future the Fennelly family might consider forming a committee with others that will help and assist them in their efforts to preserve this sacred ground.

The County Scheme
During the War of Independence, county or Amalgamation Schemes re-organised the local health infrastructure. Under the Laois County Scheme, which came into operation on 1st of May 1921, Mountmellick workhouse became the county home and the infirmary of the Abbeyleix workhouse became a district hospital. A county hospital was established in the old County infirmary at Portlaoise. The County Scheme Order provided the county home should cater for elderly and infirm persons, chronic invalids, epileptics and idiots. 'The Commission of the Relief of the Sick and Destitute Poor', who visited the county in the mid-1920s, found that there were also in-residence unmarried mothers, lunatics and children. The County Hospital operated in conjunction with the district hospital in Abbeyleix. The county hospital dealt with the more acute and serious operation cases from all parts of the county. They noted that provision for maternity cases for respectable women was made in the Abbeyleix hospital and three wards on the female side were set aside for infectious disease cases.

The Old Abbeyleix Infirmary
The Old Abbeyleix Infirmary or Workhouse was built from the profits of the 'Abbeyleix Loan Fund.' It was built on part of the present-day Council yard and faced out towards the Ballinakill road. The workhouse was run by the sisters of Charity, St Vincent de Paul. Sister Louise Madden, a Tipperary woman, was in charge of the female ward, when an allegation was made against her and the Catholic Chaplain for the workhouse Rev, James Lalor, PP.

Proselytism
Proselytism is the act of religious conversion. It can be seen as a form of involuntary forced conversion through bribery,

coercion, or violence. Proselytism is illegal. Both Sister Louise and the Chaplain allegedly tried to interfere with the religion of a Protestant patient named Bridget Taylor. They were accused of trying to convert her from her Protestant religion to that of a Roman Catholic while she lay dying in her bed in the workhouse on the 19th of June 1909. The Board of Guardians decided to hold a Sworn Inquiry at a later date to determine the matter. The result of the 'enquiry' is not known, however they both remained on in their positions. Sister Louise Madden died in the workhouse from pneumonia at the age of 63 years on April the 16th 1920 after 31 years vocation. Fr James Lalor PP of Abbeyleix died on the 2nd of March 1919 aged 75 years. Sister Josephine Buckley, a native of Cork, belonged to the order of the Sisters of Charity, St Vincent de Paul. She took up duty in the workhouse in the 1890s, she too died there at the age of 65 years on the 30 April 1931. Sister Josephine died of cardiac disease. She was in her 47th year of religious vocation, after having spent over 30 years there in the workhouse. Both sisters were interred in the Roman Catholic Church graveyard in Abbeyleix. The Master of the workhouse at the time was Michael Maher, who lived in the workhouse along with his wife and one son named John Patrick. The Matron of the workhouse was Sister Joanna Kavanagh aged 26 years as stated on the 1911 census.

Change On the Way
When the first Irish Free State Government formed in 1922, the stigma of the workhouse began to change. The workhouse itself had already had its name changed to the 'Abbeyleix District Hospital' in 1921. The paupers in this place were relieved when the tobacco rules were changed and were allowed to buy a penny's worth of "Goms." Goms were pieces of tobacco that was left over after cutting the tobacco. If the paupers had a penny, they could purchase the tobacco in Daniel Cass's shop that was situated close to the workhouse.

In 1934, the hospital was demolished. The cut stone, taken down one stone at a time, was reused to build an extension to the Patrician Brothers school at the North end of the town. The extension was to cater for the living quarters of the Brothers. When the workhouse was demolished, a stone that had been incorporated into the building and bore an inscription and date was taking to the de Vesci family Estate for safe keeping and is now in the possession of Thomas, 7th Viscount de Vesci who fortunately has a great interest in the Historical Heritage of Abbeyleix. When the old Hospital was demolished, one of the wings was retained and used as a General and Maternity ward until it too was demolished in 1964. Most births up to this time of course were home births. Baby's that were born in the old Abbeyleix District Hospital were born under the guidance of Nurse O' Shea. The first recorded birth was on the 3rd of April 1924 and the last recorded one was on the 6th of July 1962.

The New Fever Hospital

Construction on the new Fever hospital began in 1934 and opened in 1936 at a cost of £50,000. The walls and floors of the hospital were completed in Terrazzo by the Rocco family who came from Italy and eventually settled in Ireland when the work was completed. This hospital was staffed by the sisters of the little company of Mary, or otherwise known as the Blue Nuns. The Sisters of Charity had been recalled back to their Mother-House. The district hospital, or what was left, continued to operate from the older building at this time.

By the late 1940s, the Fever Hospital had a 104-bed capacity, including a sanatorium. During those early years, and in a bid to keep the running costs of the hospital down to a minimum, pigs were kept at the back of the hospital and fed on the offal that was created daily after all the patients were fed. Of course, at this time most households around the town kept pigs which helped the people provide for their families. The pigs when fattened were sold off at the pig fair that was held in the town on the first Monday of every month. Heating for the hospital was provided by way of a boiler house situated to the rear of the building, operated by men from Abbeyleix like James Carroll from New Row, James Moore from Cappnaclough, James Fennelly from Rathmoyle, Tommy Wallace from Ballypickas, Joe Mc Grath from Rathmoyle and Gerry Kavanagh from Thornberry.

Bill Cummins was the caretaker of the local dispensary, porter, and gardener. He took up the position in October 1927. At his retirement, after 36 years of work, Bill had worked under ten different Matrons. He had seen six different Medical Officers in the District Hospital. At 71 years of age, Bill remembered the old Workhouse being demolished and a new one built to replace it. He also remembered the departure of the Sisters of Charity from Abbeyleix, succeeded by a staff of lay nurses. He could still recall the arrival of the Blue Sisters in 1937 and their departure 20 years later.

By the late 1950s, the number of infectious cases had decreased dramatically and it was decided to turn the new fever hospital into a general district and maternity one. In 1955, Abbeyleix woman Mrs Joe Maher became the first S.R.N. or state registered nurse to take up duty in the hospital. Her name was Phil Maher nee Mc Grath. Sadly, Phil passed away at the very young age of 49 on the 31st of October 1982. The first Matron to take charge of the hospital in 1956 was Ms Teresa Doyle who hailed from Tullamore in county Offaly. Teresa remained Matron in charge up until she retired from her post in 1977 after serving 21 years. The Blue Nuns had retired from their role in the Hospital in 1960.

The youngest Matron in the country succeeded Teresa Doyle, when she took charge of the Abbeyleix hospital in 1977. Her name was Anne Doherty who came all the way from Longford. Anne remained in charge up until she retired in 2005 after serving almost 29 years in her role. Anne could write a book herself about her experience, recalling what she witnessed and experienced during her long career serving as Matron of Abbeyleix Hospital! I am glad to say that Anne is really enjoying her retirement now. Anne also happens to be an avid golfer and is a valued member of the Abbeyleix Golf Club. Following Annes retirement Mrs Mary Lawlor assumed the role of Director of Nursing at the Hospital. Dolores Flaherty is presently the Person in Charge. Abbeyleix District Hospital underwent a name change in the early 2000s and is now known as the Abbeyleix Community Nursing Unit. Amazingly the Poor Law Union Books for Abbeyleix from 1844-1919 and the minute books for the Abbeyleix District Hospital, 1930-1961 still exist in the County Library today. It is so important that we protect our past for the future.

A Final Thank You

James G Carroll and I would very much like to thank Mary Margaret Daly the person that has overseen this Unit in Abbeyleix from 2019 up to the present time. We both agree that we need people like this with a vision for the future, someone that can see the benefit of completing such a project for future generations to enjoy. My overall feeling now after having written this story is one of sadness. The only link that the Abbeyleix people now have with the notorious workhouse that operated here from 1842 up until conditions changed somewhat in 1922 is one of a deafening silence. It's a feeling that you get when you stand inside the gates of the pauper's graveyard or the Shank-Yard. It's the haunting feeling when you realize that you are standing on the graveyard pit where thousands of poor unfortunate destitute people were thrown into a hole, covered up and forgotten about. I would feel much more aligned with these people here rather than the ones that had the power but choose to stand idly by.

Acknowledgements

I wish to acknowledge the help and information that I received from people too numerous to mention while compiling this book. If there is anyone whom I have omitted in my thanks, I ask their forgiveness.

The Peoples Poet, John Keegan, Henry Wadsworth Longfellow, W. F. Holmes, National Photographic, Archive, National Library of Ireland, Cannon O Hanlon, Irish news archives, (Sinead) Library Archives Portlaoise, 7th Viscount Tom De Vesci, Knapton, Lal Deegan, Dáithi Ó Bricli, Karen Ryan, Old Town, Patricia Mc Cabe, Ballyragget, Teresa Sheeran, Rathmoyle, Anthony Tynan, Raheen, Margaret Kenny, Grawn Attanagh, Mick Hopper Delaney, Rathmoyle, John Murphy, Rathmoyle, Annette Duff, Éamonn an Chnoíc Mike Rafter, Quite County, Martin Fennelly, Rathmoyle, Mary Carroll Knapton, Marie Mullally, Balladine, Geraldine O Keeffe, Lower Boley Shanahoe, Sean Carroll, Sweet-view Abbeyleix. John Galvin, Colt, Gerard O Hara, Laburnum Close, Andrew Bennett, Sweet-view, George & Peter Dobb's, Liverpool & Belfast, Patrick Begadon, Aughmacart, Peter & Andrea Rogers, Killamuck, Seanie O Neill, Spink, FR. Paddy Byrne PP, Abbeyleix, Tom Kelly, Killamuck. Richard Kennedy, Ralish, John Moore, Ballinakill Road, Jack Nolan, Ballymullen Abbeyleix. Aillie Holsford, Dublin. and Laurence Kavanagh, Ballymaddock. Eugene Fennelly. Abbeyleix Heritage House. Don't forget, edited by Ruby Eyre.

About The Author

Noel Burke has a keen interest in local history and dedicates a lot of his time to research. Now that he has reached his pension aged years, he also spends a lot of his time in the archival research library. He loves spending time with his Grandchildren and living here in his native Heritage Town of Abbeyleix along with his wife Patricia.

Thank You

If you enjoyed this book, please leave a review online and spread the word! I am also on Facebook where I share more stories, photographs and videos of Abbeyleix and its people.

(Pictured: Author's Granddaughter, Jessica Whelan, Book Cover designer)

Printed in Great Britain
by Amazon

15265489R00129